Sew, Craft, Quilt and Embroider Confidently

with Sulky® Stabilizers

A complete guide to using Stabilizers for professional results.

by Joyce Drexler

Dedicated to my Mother - Mary Ann Menke Billow,
who taught me that anything is possible.

Contents

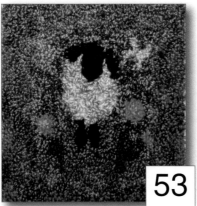

39

53

71

109

Sulky Iron-on Transfer Pens

117

Quilting - Made Easy with Stabilizers

121

Embroidery - Made Easy with Stabilizers

153

CD - in the back of this book

Patterns for Projects, over 6 Bonus Projects & Sewing Stars' Food Recipes

190

Introduction

Since so many of you have told us that you want to understand and properly use stabilizers in your sewing, crafting, quilting and embroidering, Sulky asked me to create this comprehensive book to be your guide to achieve professional results every time.

Through the years, you have seen me, along with many of our National Sulky Educators, via PBS TV Shows like: Sewing with Nancy; America Sews with Sue Hausmann; Fons & Porter; Kaye Wood's Quilting Friends; Sew Creative; America Quilts Creatively; Quilting Arts; Martha's Sewing Room and others. In years past, many of you ordered products from my Speed Stitch Catalog or attended my Speed Stitch Success Seminars and S.M.A.R.T seminars in the 80's or 90's, or now attend Sulky Certified Teacher Trainings or Sulky "Sew Exciting™" Seminars.

I recall when I first started free-motion embroidering in 1977, long before home computerized embroidery machines were invented, I was so excited when I first discovered and packaged Sulky Solvy Stabilizer --- a water soluble. It was like magic how it dissolved in water! It made monogramming, cut-work, lace-work and 3-D applique so much easier. And now, all these years later, there are 19 Sulky Stabilizers to choose from. Now, any garment, craft project, quilt or embroidery can be expertly done with professional results every time! With the availability of so many magnificent colors of Sulky Threads in the highest quality Rayon, Polyester, Metallic, Cotton and Blendables™, your efforts are beautifully rewarded.

With this book you will learn **everything** you need to know to choose the correct stabilizer for any project you undertake. We've done the experimenting and have learned a lot, and in this book you will benefit from our mistakes and challenges --- to shorten your learning curve. Time is precious. This book is designed to help you achieve the professional results you have always longed for without spending any of your precious time and money on trial and error.

Each stabilizer is explained in detail. Use this book as a reference and as a source of inspiration. Projects featuring every Sulky Stabilizer are also included to add to your fun and growth in machine arts and crafts.

Be sure to visit www.sulky.com for even more information, color thread charts and lots more, including FREE projects! Check out our new Embroidery Club with designs from Carol Ingram and me. Plus, be sure to sign up for my informative and FREE Monthly Newsletter.

Create with Confidence,

Joyce Drexler

Joyce Drexler
Author, Artist, Designer,
T.V. Personality and
co-founder of
Sulky of America

Enjoy Sulky's Newest Stabilizers!

Sulky has introduced 2 new stabilizers since we published the hugely popular, **"An Updated Supplement to Sulky's Secrets to Successful Stabilizing"** - Book 900B-17, and a total of 9 new stabilizers since we published,

"Sulky Secrets to Successful Stabilizing" - Book #900B-11. The two newest ones are:

Cut-Away Stabilizer:
- **Soft 'n Sheer Extra™**

Water Soluble Stabilizer:
- **Sticky Fabri-Solvy™**

It has always been our goal at Sulky to bring you the most pertinent information you need to be successful using Sulky products in all of your fun and creative sewing, embroidery, quilting, and crafting projects.

Consistently high quality Sulky Stabilizers are the only ones you will ever need to "Create with Confidence".

- Sulky Stabilizers are made using a combination of the most advanced technology and the highest quality, fiber-based materials. All are acid-free and lead-free.
- No other Stabilizers have more fibers per square inch.
- All Sulky 8", 12" and 20" rolls are packaged in a reusable storage container to keep them fresh and usable for years.
- All Sulky Stabilizers have color-coded packaging and icons to help you choose the right Sulky Stabilizer for each of your creative projects.
- Clear, easy-to-understand directions in every package assure success every time.
- Go to **www.sulky.com** for a vast pool of knowledge about Sulky Stabilizers.
- For almost 30 years, millions of consumers have relied on the uncompromising quality of Sulky products.

The CD in the back of this book contains:

- Patterns for all of the projects included in this book.
- Great Food Recipes from your favorite Sewing Stars!
- Terrific Bonus Projects.

As time goes by, we will undoubtedly invent more new products to make all of your creative projects even easier, so stay in touch.

We know you will find even more creative uses for all of our quality stabilizers.

Give us your ideas and questions by e-mailing asksulky@sulky.com

Check out our "Frequently Asked Questions and Answers" section anytime of the day or night at:

www.sulky.com

Sulky Cut-Away Permanent Stabilizers

You can cut or burn them away, and dye, paint, stamp or embroider on them! Sulky Cut-Away, permanent Stabilizers are a must-have!

What are non-woven, Sulky "Cut-Away" Stabilizers made of?

Cut-Away Plus™ is made of 10% Cellulose/Viscose and 90% Polyester. **Soft 'n Sheer™** and the newer **Soft 'n Sheer Extra™** are made of 100% Continuous Filament Nylon and Polyethylene Copolymers. **Tender Touch™** and **Fuse 'n Stitch™** are both 100% Polyester and they have a fusible, iron-on backing. All are lead-free, acid-free and non-woven, and they provide excellent uniform coverage. **Soft 'n Sheer also comes in black.**

When and how do I use these different Permanent Stabilizers?

Use them anywhere a permanent stabilizer is needed to provide ongoing stability through washing and wearing. Typically, when embroidering stretchy or knitted fabrics with densely digitized or free-motion embroidery designs, **Cut-Away Plus** is recommended for heavier knits like sweatshirts, whereas **Soft 'n Sheer** is used when embroidering lightweight knits like T-shirts and sweaters. Soft 'n Sheer is also ideal for making free-standing appliqués. **Sulky Soft 'n Sheer Extra** is 1-1/2 times as heavy as original Soft 'n Sheer with the added convenience of having a fusible, iron-on backing.

Tender Touch is a lightweight, permanent stabilizer that is ideal to "cover-the-back" of finished embroideries to protect sensitive skin from scratchy stitches. Also use it as an interfacing for delicate fabrics like silk, satin, lamé, batiste, open-weave wovens, and lightweight cottons, and to protect lightweight, delicate fabrics by giving them needed support while embroidering, without changing the hand or drape of the fabric. (See package instructions for additional stabilizing instructions.) It is ideal for baby and children's garments, sports apparel, lingerie, spandex and golf shirts because it stretches with the garment.

Fuse 'n Stitch is ideal for projects that need extra stiffness and retained support. Iron it in place wherever a permanent interfacing might be used. Ideal for continuous hoop embroidery, tote bags, lamp shades, purses, belts, book covers, wallhangings, and more.

Beautiful Dyed Cut-Away Plus Project by Carol Ingram on p. 55.

Use Cut-Away Plus as an Art Canvas ...

Since it is a very firm but soft and absorbent substance, many artists use Cut-Away Plus as a canvas because it is inexpensive but reacts well to paint, dye, fabric inks and stamps. The project above can be found on page 55, and the one below is on the CD found in the back of this book. Also a great idea for journal covers.

Dyed Cut-Away Plus S.W. Scene by Carol Ingram on CD.

Use Soft 'n Sheer and Soft 'n Sheer Extra as Support Stabilizers that are permanent...

Provides great permanent stability on lightweight knits and wovens for digitized and free-motion embroidery designs, appliqués, and monograms. Perfect for dense embroidery designs, open-weave fabrics, or lightweight fabrics with a complex design.

Ideal for trapunto, for lining pillows, and for backing fabrics that tend to get caught on or in the throat plate of the machine while free-motion stitching.

With excellent stretch resistance, Soft 'n Sheer Extra eliminates pulling or sagging from the surrounding fabric not only during the stitching process, but during washing and wearing.

www.sulky.com - "Angel Collection" by Joyce Drexler

Use Soft 'n Sheer as a foundation for free-standing appliqués ...

Use Soft 'n Sheer as a foundation fabric on which to build embroideries. Then, burn away the excess for making ornaments, appliqués, patches, etc. A great way to make good use of a test-stitch-out of an embroidery design is to do it on Soft 'n Sheer, then burn away the excess and you have an embroidered appliqué (like the teddy bear below) that can be stitched on anything. Perfect for stabilizing T-shirt quilts and soft enough to remain within the quilt without making it stiff.

www.sulky.com - "Teatime Teddies Collection" by Carol Ingram

Use Cut-Away Plus and Fuse 'n Stitch as Quilt and Appliqué Templates ...

To make quilting and appliqué templates, use Sulky Iron-On, Permanent Transfer Pens to transfer designs multiple times onto these permanent stabilizers. You can use multiple layers to make your template as thick as needed for your project. Saves time and money compared to using plastic templates.

An Amy Butler Design - sewn by Nancy Estep. See page 31.

Use Fuse 'n Stitch and Tender Touch as Iron-on Interfacings ...

Use Fuse 'n Stitch when you need firm stiffness, like in purse handles, belts, waistbands, hats, totes, etc. Starting on page 71, you will see how we used it for corded, embroidered trivets, frames and more. Use Tender Touch for facings on jacket lapels, and for creating facings when making sweatshirt jackets from pullover sweatshirts, etc.

Use Tender Touch as a Cover-up ...

Over the underside of embroidery stitches to prevent scratchy irritation. Ideal for children's and baby clothing and for anyone who has sensitive skin. For a more finished look, use a scallop-edge or wavy-blade cutter when cutting the Tender Touch. If desired, you can give Tender Touch a shot of steam before ironing it down to pre-shrink it.

Use Tender Touch as a Block-out ...

On lightweight or light-colored fabrics that you want to use as appliqué pieces on darker fabric, iron Tender Touch on the back before cutting and appliquéing to both block out the color underneath and stabilize the fabric from fraying, etc.

Dye or Stamp Cut-Away Plus to use as fabric.

Tender Touch

Available Put-ups:
275-01 - 20" x 1 yd. Package
275-08 - 7 2/3" x 9 yd. Roll
275-25 - 20" x 25 yd. Bolt.

Sulky Cut-Away Plus™

This **permanent**, mid-weight, non-woven stabilizer is as soft as it is strong. It provides great **permanent** stability to stitch computerized embroidery designs, appliqués, and monograms on outerwear like jackets, sweaters and sweatshirts. Ideal for open-weave fabrics with a complex design, high detail embroidery designs, or dense designs.

Cut-Away Plus is sheer enough so it doesn't show through most fabrics when the excess is trimmed away. It supports through the stitching process and continues to support through washing and wearing. It is both washable and dry-cleanable.

Experiment with different combinations on different weights or types of fabric. Sometimes using Cut-Away Plus along with one or more other Sulky Stabilizers does the best job.

Use Cut-Away Plus to make an art project like a cover for a book, album or journal. It's fun to use for paper dolls and their clothing since it can be dyed, painted, stamped, etc. You can even use it as a lightweight batting in clothing and wall-hangings.

Modeled by: Abigail Prater.

Sulky Soft 'n Sheer™

*An ultra-soft, textured, **permanent** cut-away stabilizer. Provides great permanent stability to stitch computerized embroidery designs, appliqués, and monograms on lightweight knits and wovens. Ideal for dense embroidery designs, open-weave fabrics, or lightweight fabrics with a complex design. Ideal for trapunto and free-form appliqués of thread like those shown below.*

With excellent stretch resistance, Soft 'n Sheer eliminates pulling or sagging from the surrounding fabric not only during the stitching process, but during washing and wearing. Since Soft 'n Sheer is made from nylon it does not tolerate a hot iron. Use a low temperature setting and a press cloth.

When stitching is completed, clip away all the loose bobbin threads, then cut away any excess stabilizer from around the outside of the embroideries. The stabilizer inside the stitched design will remain to act as a permanent stabilizer to support the embroidery through washing and wearing. If using more than one layer, and if you want a smoother finish, you can "grade" the layers using pinking shears.

This is a very versatile stabilizer.

Available White Put-ups:
235-01 - 20" x 1 yd. Package
235-03 - 20" x 3 yd. Package
235-08 - 8" x 11 yd. Roll
235-12 - 12" x 11 yd. Roll
235-20 - 20" x 5 yd. Roll
235-25 - 20" x 25 yd. Bolt.

Available Black Put-ups:
236-01 - 20" x 1 yd. Package
236-08 - 8" x 11 yd. Roll
236-12 - 12" x 11 yd. Roll
236-25 - 20" x 25 yd. Bolt

You can make free-form appliqués by trimming the Soft'n Sheer to about 1/8" and then burning the excess away with a stencil cutter or wood-burning tool.

Sulky Soft 'n Sheer Extra™

Just like the original Soft 'n Sheer but half again as heavy, and it has a fusible coating on the back. This makes it ideal for hooped embroidery where you need a lightweight, stretch-resistant stabilizer that you can simply iron onto your garment. Great for open-weave sweaters and other stretchy knits.

Available Put-ups:
237-01 - 20" x 1 yd. Package
237-08 - 8" x 9 yd. Roll
237-12 - 12" x 9 yd. Roll
237-25 - 20" x 25 yd. Bolt

Cassie Genawese is wearing a "Maidenhair Fern" embroidery design from Joyce Drexler's "Jumbo Ferns" Collection - www.sulky.com.

Sulky Tender Touch™

Tender Touch is a lightweight, permanent, iron-on stabilizer that is ideal to "cover the back" of finished, computerized or free-motion embroideries or decorative stitches to protect sensitive skin from scratchy stitches. It can also be used as the first step in stabilizing delicate fabrics like batiste, satin, lamé, silk, open-weave wovens and lightweight cottons to help prevent shredding or distortion due to heavy needle penetrations when embroidering. When used as an interfacing in garment construction and fabric manipulation, it does not change the hand or drape of the fabric.

Available Put-ups:
664-01 - 20" x 1 yd. Package
664-08 - 8" x 9 yd. Roll
664-25 - 20" x 25 yd. Bolt

www.sulky.com - "Inspirational Concepts"; by Joyce Drexler for Great Embroidery.

7 *Cut-Away Stabilizers*

Sulky Fuse 'n Stitch™

A permanent, crisp, heavyweight, iron-on stabilizer. Ideal for projects that need extra stiffness and retained support. Also, iron in place wherever a permanent interfacing might be used.

Perfect for continuous-hoop embroidery, tote bags, lamp shades, purses, bookcovers, pinwoven portraits, photo frames, trivets, placemats, journals, pockets, collars, facings, belts, scrapbooking and wallhangings.

Available Put-ups:

663-01 - 20" x 1 yd. Package
663-08 - 8" x 9 yd. Roll
663-20 - 20" x 5 yd. Roll
663-25 - 24" x 25 yd. Bolt

Photo Pin-weaving from the book, **"An Updated Supplement to Sulky's Secrets to Successful Stabilizing".**

www.sulky.com - "Jumbo Ferns" embroidery designs by Joyce Drexler

Cut-Away **8**
Stabilizers

Sulky Water Soluble Stabilizers

They are Magical! They disappear! Since the first Sulky Solvy was introduced in the U.S.A. and Canada in 1983, they have revolutionized Machine Arts and Crafts.

What are Sulky "Solvy" Stabilizers made of?

All, except Paper Solvy, are water soluble, temporary stabilizers or transfer agents which are made of polyvinyl alcohol so they dissolve in water like magic! Super Solvy is twice as thick, heavy and strong as the original Sulky Solvy, while Ultra Solvy is four times as thick. All are non-toxic and resistant to organic materials such as fats, oils, etc. They will dissolve in water with a temperature of anywhere from 32° to 200°. To make **Solvy or Super Solvy** thicker and firmer, two or more layers can be fused together either by layering them and applying a warm iron for several seconds or by lightly misting one layer with water and smoothing another layer over it.

Paper Solvy™ is a combination of polyvinyl alcohol and wood pulp which makes it look, feel and behave like paper, but it still washes out in water. It can be used in either an ink-jet printer or bubble-jet printer, but laser printers get too hot. Paper Solvy generally washes out very quickly in warm water. HOWEVER, because there is a wood pulp component, it is very important to THOROUGHLY rinse the item THE FIRST TIME until there is no slippery residue or tiny bits of the Paper Solvy remaining. Otherwise, if there is some product remaining, it will likely be the wood pulp, which will be next to impossible to remove once dry. Tiny stitches make it harder for the wood pulp to be released. To assure precise results, always test on a separate sample of your project.

Fabri-Solvy™ is an innovative addition to the Sulky Solvy line of wash-away stabilizers. This unique product has the firmness and feel of fabric thus allowing a multitude of possible applications. You will fall in love with its non-woven strength and quality for computer embroidery, cut-work, lace making and appliqué. It washes away easily, placing no stress on your beautiful thread work.

When & How do I use the different Solvy Stabilizers?

Use them anywhere that dissolving the stabilizer would be preferable to tearing, cutting or heating it away. All are widely used in the following applications: quilting, computerized embroidery, lace work, buttonholes, thread sketching, foundation piecing, edgework, charted needlework, cut-work, monogramming, free-motion lace, thread scarves, 3-D appliqué, shadow work, heirloom sewing, battenburg lace, smocking, hand-turned appliqué, serger lace, as a reinforcement for sewing on lightweight and sheer fabrics, as a topper on toweling and knits, and much more.

Use Solvys as a Foundation ...
Ultra Solvy and Fabri-Solvy have the firmness that is required when creating free-motion thread lace, battenburg lace, digitized lace and cut-work.

From the "Jumbo Ferns" Collection
by Joyce Drexler. www.sulky.com

Use Solvy or Super Solvy as a Topper...

Solvy and Super Solvy are perfect not only as a topper on napped fabrics like towels to keep the loops or piles from poking through the stitching, but also to prevent stitches from getting lost in the fabric, and to enhance the clarity of fine lettering and detail stitching. They are not recommended for non-washable velvet.

When quilting raw-edged, appliquéd quilts like those by McKenna Ryan and Maggie Walker, cover the entire quilt top with Solvy while quilting. When finished, simply wash the quilt to remove the Solvy.

Solvy and Super Solvy are also very helpful when felting and stitching over loose fibers.

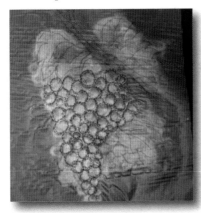

Use all Solvys For Tracing ...

For handling ease, place the design under any Solvy (except Paper Solvy) which is secured in a hoop, or lightly spray the pattern with Sulky KK 2000 and smooth the Solvy over it to keep it from shifting while tracing. Trace it with an extra-fine, permanent-ink marker or a wash-out or disappearing ink marker, depending on the color of thread and fabric to be used. Iron-on transfers made with a Sulky Iron-On Transfer Pen can be ironed onto **Solvy, Super Solvy or Fabri-Solvy** *with a dry iron (NO STEAM).*

Use Paper Solvy For Printing Paper Piecing ...

and for retrieving designs off your computer or the internet. Quickly print one or more copies of a design on Paper Solvy and have it wash out once it's stitched. You can either print multiple copies of designs in copy machines or through ink-jet or bubble-jet printers; trace designs using permanent-ink markers or pencils; or heat-transfer designs using Sulky Iron-on Transfer Pens. Make larger pieces by adhering two or more pieces together with Sulky KK 2000 or water soluble tape. Perfect for Paper Piecing!

Solvys as Liquid ...

Brush them on as a liquid stabilizer made by dissolving in 8 oz. of water:
• 1 yd. of Solvy, or
• 1/2 yard of **Super Solvy**, or
• 1/4 yd. of **Ultra Solvy**

This is not a finite recipe. Many people just save their scraps in a jar with water to which they add more Solvy (or dilute with water) to get the desired consistency for their next project. Store unused portion in a sealed, labeled container in the refrigerator. Brush it on fabric using a bristle brush or foam brush. When it dries, it stiffens and stabilizes your fabric so it can be embellished without hooping. Brush it on to stabilize the areas where you will stitch buttonholes.

Brush a thicker solution on the inside of felted bowls (*see Book #900B-17 - "An Updated Supplement to Sulky's Secrets to Successful Stabilizing"*) to help them retain their shape and stiffness, and to re-form and re-stiffen thread lace bowls (*see Book #900B-15 "Sulky's Secrets to Successful Embroidery"*).

Great for use with quilter's cotton when embroidering quilts so you will have absolutely no puckers! (*See Book #900B-16, "Quick & Easy Weekend Quilting with Sulky"* for a beautifully embroidered floral quilt.)

Adhering Solvys to Fabrics ...

Spray Sulky **KK 2000** onto the fabric, or mist the fabric with water, then finger-press the Solvy onto it. (To create larger pieces of Ultra Solvy, moisten one edge with a sponge and overlap another piece of it onto the moistened edge. Let dry.) Because KK-2000 is NOT water soluble, it will not wash out with water. It needs to dissipate into the fibers. For techniques like making scarves with yarns and ribbons, when KK 2000 is sprayed between two layers of Solvy or Super Solvy you need to help it dissipate before wetting by pressing your finished "sandwich" with a warm, dry iron. Otherwise, you may end up with some sticky residue (which should come out easily with denatured alcohol or rubbing alcohol - color-test first). Note: If your iron does not have a non-stick surface, be sure to use a press cloth.

Removal of Solvy is Easy ...

Once stitching is completed, carefully trim or tear away excess **Solvy,** then put a damp press cloth on the remaining Solvy. Press with a warm, dry iron. Any Solvy that remains can be removed by submerging the project in cool or warm water for 3 to 5 minutes. **Rinse thoroughly.** Air dry on a towel.

It may take a little longer to dissolve Solvy that has been layered together or when using any of the heavier Solvys; additional clear water rinsing may be needed. When working with a large project or the heavier Solvys, it is best to fill a top-loading washer with water, place the project in the washer, and allow it to agitate for 5-10 minutes. (Put delicate items in a lingerie bag.) Remove it to dry. Then, add detergent and launder a load of clothes. When **Paper Solvy or Fabri-Solvy** are submerged in water by themselves, they disappear within 10 seconds (but longer rinsing for a project is recommended).

How should I store Solvys? ...

Store unused portions in a sealed zip-lock bag. Store unused liquid Solvy in a sealed, labeled jar in the refrigerator. Store rolls in a zip-lock bag inside the plastic container that it comes in. In dry climates, if not stored properly, **Solvy, Super Solvy and Ultra Solvy** can become brittle, but they are still useable. In damp climates they can become soft and sticky, so it is best to use them in an air conditioned environment. **Fabri-Solvy** does not react to climate conditions - except rain of course!

Sulky Solvy™

The perfect, see-through, lightweight stabilizer and transfer agent that dissolves in water. Use as a design template, as a pattern guide and as a stitch support. This lightest weight Solvy pulls away from stitching and releases easily with just a gentle pull, or by applying a damp Q-Tip. **Ideal when you do not want any stabilizer to show on the top or bottom.**

Available Put-ups:

486-01 - 19-3/4" x 1 yd. Package
486-03 - 19-1/2" x 3 yd. Package
486-08 - 8" x 9 yd. Roll
486-12 - 12" x 9 yd. Roll
486-25 - 19-3/4" x 25 yd. Bolt

Sulky Super Solvy™

Twice as thick, heavy and strong as the original Sulky Solvy. Although both may be used interchangeably for some applications, when you need a heavier Solvy that will withstand a lot of stitching or tugging, then Super Solvy is the perfect choice. A firm, see-through stabilizer. Perfect as a topper, pattern guide, or as a backing stabilizer. Use as a design template, as a pattern guide and as a stitch support. Ideal when you to not want any stabilizer to show on the top or bottom.

Available Put-ups:

405-01 - 20" x 1 yd. Package
405-08 - 8" x 9 yd. Roll
405-12 - 12" x 9 yd. Roll
405-25 - 20" x 25 yd. Bolt

Thread Bowls
from the book, "*Sulky Secrets to Successful Embroidery*".

Sulky Ultra Solvy™

Very firm, 4 times as heavy as the original Solvy. Great for: Hoopless Embroidery, Computerized Lace, Computerized Embroidery, Free-Motion Embroidery, Quilt Patterns, Lace Work, Buttonholes, Edge Work, Thread Sketching, 3-D Embroidery Designs, Cut Work, Monogramming, Thread Lace, 3-D Appliqué and Shadow Work.

Available Put-ups:

408-01 - 20" x 1 yd. Package
408-03 - 19-1/2" x 3 yd. Package
408-08 - 8" x 8 yd. Roll
408-12 - 12" x 8 yd. Roll
408-25 - 20" x 25 yd. Bolt

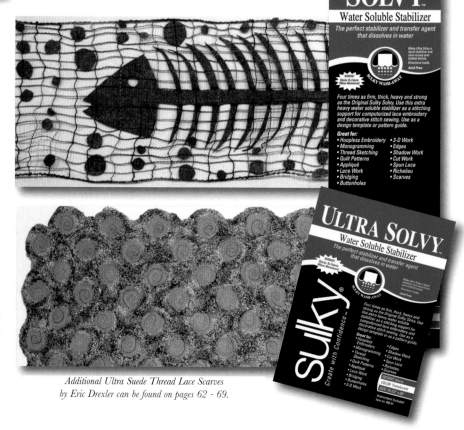

Additional Ultra Suede Thread Lace Scarves
by Eric Drexler can be found on pages 62 - 69.

Sulky Paper Solvy™

Washes out in water in seconds!

A great way to use designs off your computer or the internet. Quickly print one or more copies of a design onto Paper Solvy and have it wash out once it's stitched.

Use Paper Solvy as a base or backing, with or without printing a design on it. Great for: Paper-pieced Quilting Designs, Appliqué, Foundation Piecing, Sashiko, Counted Cross Stitch and more!

You can either: print multiple copies of designs in copy machines, ink-jet or bubble-jet printers; trace designs onto it using pencils or permanent-ink markers; or heat transfer designs onto it using Sulky Iron-on Transfer Pens. Make larger pieces by adhering the ends of two pieces together with Sulky KK 2000 Temporary Spray Adhesive or water soluble tape. *Available Put-up:* **409-02 - Twelve - 8-1/2" x 11" Sheets**

Sulky Fabri-Solvy™ and Sulky Sticky Fabri-Solvy™

Fabri-Solvy has the firmness and feel of fabric but it easily washes away, placing no stress on your beautiful thread work. It is the perfect stabilizer for doing multiple computerized embroideries because it is not affected by the heat of the machine after many hours of embroidery. Perfect for free-motion embroidery, cut-work, lace making and turned appliqué.

Fabri-Solvy Available Put-ups:
407-01 - 20" x 1 yd. Package
407-08 - 8" x 9 yd. Roll
407-20 - 19-1/2" x 5 yd. Roll
407-25 - 20" x 25 yd. Bolt

Sticky Fabri-Solvy works just the same only it has a self-stick back which is accessed by removing a release sheet. It's like magic for turned appliqués: Stitch it, turn it, and stick it. It holds items in place for hoopless and reversible embroidery. Ideal for accurate placement of loose items when making scarves or thread collages. Photocopy your designs onto it, then **peel** off the release sheet and **stick** the design in place for hand embroidery, appliqué, needlepunch, machine and hand quilting. With no paper component, it washes away quickly and completely every time! For your photocopying convenience, it also comes in 8-1/2" x 11" sheets.

Sticky Fabri-Solvy Available Put-ups:
457-01 - 20" x 1 yd. Package
457-02 - (12) 8-1/2" x 11" Sheets
457-08 - 8" x 6 yd. Roll
457-12 - 12" x 6 yd. Roll
457-25 - 20" x 25 yd. Bolt

Sulky Tear-Away Stabilizers

What are Sulky "Tear-Away", Stabilizers made of?

Tear-Easy ™ is a soft, lightweight, temporary stabilizer that is made of 100% Cellulose/Viscose and has a definite grain. It can be torn in straight strips in one direction.

Stiffy™ is a crisp, firm, medium-weight, temporary stabilizer that is used when a heavier tear-away is preferred. It is made of 35% Cellulose/Viscose and 65% Polyester.

Totally Stable™ is a medium-weight, iron-on, temporary stabilizer that is coated on one side so it can be temporarily fused to a fabric to eliminate shifting, sliding, puckering and stretching of that fabric while it is being stitched. It can be peeled up and repositioned many times. It is also used in quilting as a pattern and/or template, and as a backing for free-motion quilting. It is 18% Polyester and 82% Cellulose/Viscose.

Sticky+™ is a self-adhesive, non-woven, temporary stabilizer that is super easy to use as a hooping aid and stabilizer. Using Sticky+ saves time and provides great stability combined with effortless removal, and it doesn't gum up your needle. It is intended for use on the wrong side of the fabric. It is also widely used as a backing when painting T-shirts, etc., because it keeps the paint from bleeding through and keeps the knit on grain and stable while painting. It is 100% Cellulose /Viscose.

All Sulky tear-aways are phthalate-free, acid-free and non-woven, and they don't stretch in any direction. They provide excellent stability through the stitching process, and they tear away easily once stitching is completed.

When & How do I use these different Tear-Away Stabilizers?

Use tear-away stabilizers as backings for all types of appliqué, digitized and free-motion embroidery, edge stitch support, monogramming, buttonholes and decorative stitching.

With very few exceptions, even the most stunning design or surface embellishment won't work properly unless it is stitched with the right type of stabilizer underneath that provides the stability needed to keep every stitch in place without puckering. Tear-aways are used under fabrics to prevent tunneling, distortion and puckering when you are doing techniques where removing the stabilizer by tearing will neither disturb the hand of the stitching, nor pull, distort or loosen the stitches on the edge of the design.

Check out "Embroidery Recipes" starting on page 138. You can embroider on all types of fabrics following Sulky's easy recipes.

Use Tear-Easy or Stiffy to support fabric for embroidery or appliqué ...

Tear-Easy and Stiffy are often used in combination with permanent stabilizers like Sulky Cut-Away Plus or Sulky Soft 'n Sheer when doing digitized embroidery, depending on the fabric being embroidered. Ultra stiffness in a tear-away may provide the support you need, but if it pulls out stitches when torn away, it could ruin the project. That's when layering the softer, easier-to-tear Sulky Tear-Easy (in opposite directions) can be the right choice because you can easily tear away one layer at a time. Many experts will also place one or two layers of Tear-Easy under their hooped embroidery. When doing computerized embroidery, crisp, mid-weight Sulky Stiffy is well suited to low stitch count designs with fine detail. Clarity of column (satin) stitches is enhanced with Stiffy and Tear-Easy. Always tear away one layer at a time while supporting the stitching with your fingers.

Spray Tear-Easy or Stiffy with Sulky KK 2000 Temporary Spray Adhesive to make either into a "sticky type" backing stabilizer.

1. Trace ...

a design onto see-through **Tear-Easy or Stiffy** by placing a permanent pattern under the stabilizer, then tracing it with an extra-fine, permanent-ink marker, or heat transferring the design with a Sulky Iron-on Transfer Pen. Use **Tear-Easy or Stiffy** as a design template to stitch through or as a pattern guide and stitching-support piece for monogramming or digitized machine embroidery.

2. Use as a Stabilizer ...

by placing **Tear-Easy or Stiffy** under or over the fabric or design area to be stitched (hoop optional). You may pin, baste or temporarily adhere material to them with Sulky KK 2000, if desired. For added support on delicate fabrics, use two or more layers.

3. Removal is Easy ...

once stitching is completed, gently tear away excess **Tear-Easy or Stiffy,** one layer at a time (while supporting the stitching with your other hand) to prevent the pulling, tearing or distorting of stitches that can occur when tearing away a single layer of a thicker, heavier stabilizer.

Both **Tear-Easy and Stiffy** are perfect for any project where wetting or heating is not the desired method of removal.

**Tear-Easy and Stiffy
Lightweight Tear-Away
Stabilizers are ideal for Appliqué:**

- **Bottom Layer** - One to three layers of lightweight Tear-Easy or Stiffy as a support stabilizer.
- **Top Layer** - Base or foundation fabric on which Appliqué is to be worked; place right side up with cut-out applique pieces fused, pinned or basted to it.

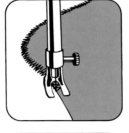

1. Thread the top and bobbin with the same color of Sulky Decorative Thread; or thread the bobbin with Sulky Polyester Invisible Thread. (Top-Stitch or Embroidery Needle recommended.) Attach an open-toe appliqué foot or free-motion darning foot on the machine.

SATIN STITCH
OR BLANKET STITCH

2. Place a piece of Tear-Easy or Stiffy (that is a few inches larger than the appliqué area) behind the base or foundation fabric. If the base or foundation

fabric is a knit or is loosely woven, for more support add one or two more layers of Tear-Easy or Stiffy, for a maximum of 3 as shown above. (If securing in a hoop --- make sure that the stabilizer is cut large enough to fit in the hoop.)

3. Use either a satin stitch, blanket stitch, decorative stitch or invisible appliqué stitch to complete the desired appliqué effect.

4. To satin stitch detail areas on a 3-D or loose appliqué, place an extra piece of Tear-Easy or Stiffy under that motif for added stability. When stopping the machine to maneuver or pivot around a corner or curve, leave the needle down in the material of the appliqué project. When fabric appliquéing, the

satin stitching line should be about 2/3 on the applique and 1/3 off the edge of the fabric.

Sticky+ is used mostly for digitized embroidery for items that can not be hooped or are too small to fit in the hoop.

- It is ideal for "hoopless embroidery" (where only the outer portion of the machine's hoop is used) because it eliminates hoop marks when embroidering on all fabrics that have a nap or a tendency to get a hoop mark, including sweatshirt fleece, Ultra Suede®, velvet, brushed velour, brushed denim, silk, flannel, knitted fabrics and caps.

- To use Sticky+, peel off and discard the paper release sheet and affix the adhesive side to the bottom of the outer portion of your hoop. Place your fabric over the hoop and finger-press to adhere it to the Sticky+. Place the hoop on the embroidery arm. If more support is needed, place a layer or two of Sulky Tear-Easy or Stiffy under the hoop, then embroider. To remove any adhesive build-up on the hoop, use Goo-Gone™, which is available at most fabric, hardware and discount stores.

- For hand work projects like counted cross-stitch, silk ribbon embroidery, etc., when the fabric isn't large enough to fit in your hoop, affix Sulky Sticky+ to the outer edges of the fabric to make it larger.

- **Using Hooped Sulky Sticky+:**

  1. Hoop Sulky Sticky+ with the release paper side up, the way you would hoop a piece of fabric.

Sticky+
Release
Sheet

  2. Using a straight pin, score the release paper.

  3. Pull it away from the adhesive layer.

4. Place the garment or fabric piece to be embroidered over the hoop. Position as desired with the grain line of the fabric straight.

Finger-press to smooth in place. The fabric can be removed and repositioned several times before Sticky+ will no longer hold.

5. Attach the Embroidery Hoop to the machine and embroider. (*Note: The inside ring of the hoop is not placed over the fabric.*)

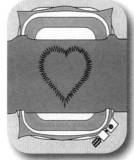

6. After the embroidery is completed, gently pull away the fabric from the Sticky+.

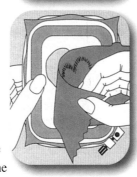

At this point, you can actually "patch" the hole in the Sticky+ in the area that was removed. Simply cut a piece of Sticky+ a little larger than the hole, remove and discard the release sheet, and stick it underneath the hole. Place the garment or fabric for the next embroidery and continue embroidering. You can continue in this manner until the Sticky+ that was originally secured in the hoop no longer holds. At that point, hoop a new piece of Sticky+ as in #1-4.

Special Tips: *Always remove the excess Sticky+ before applying heat from an iron or clothes dryer. For best results, remove excess Sticky+ from the fabric within an hour or so of application.*

You would use **Totally Stable** for stabilizing stretchy fabrics as well as lightweight woven fabrics when the fabric is suitable for ironing. Do not use on nylon or lycra because a hot iron can melt these fabrics, causing them to permanently bond with the Totally Stable. It takes very little effort to iron it in place. Just give it a quick swipe of the iron. What's really amazing about Totally Stable is the fact that you can re-iron it over and over until the fusible no longer adheres. It is perfect for making iron-on, re-useable design stitching or cutting templates, and so much more.

• To trace or transfer a design onto **Totally Stable,** place the permanent pattern under the Totally Stable and trace it with either a permanent-ink or water soluble marker. Then, iron it onto the fabric, giving you a smooth, trouble-free design pattern to follow.

• **Do not iron Totally Stable** onto fabric that has been marked with an air or water soluble marker since the heat of the iron could set the ink, making your markings permanent.

• Designs drawn or traced with a Sulky Iron-on Transfer Pen can be ironed onto **Totally Stable** either as you are adhering it to your fabric or after Totally Stable has been pressed on.

• Place the shiny, fusible side of **Totally Stable** against the wrong side of the fabric. Set your dry iron at a cotton setting and use a steady, quick ironing motion to press for several seconds. Check to see if fusing is complete. If not, apply the iron for several more seconds until **Totally Stable** is totally fused. Once the project is complete, you can easily remove the **Totally Stable** by gently peeling it up and tearing away the excess. The fabric underneath will be completely free of sticky or unsightly residue.

• If multiple rehoopings are required, the stabilizer may loosen and need to be re-ironed to re-adhere it totally.

**Use Totally Stable to make perfect Re-useable Templates for Appliqué and Quilt Pieces
as well as a Stabilizer to support stitching.**

Making various precision shapes for quilting is perfectly simple with Totally Stable because you can:

1. See through Totally Stable to trace a design onto it.
2. Iron it onto your fabric to keep the fabric from stretching and distorting as you cut out shapes. (Great for stabilizing bias cuts.)
3. Easily remove Totally Stable and iron it on again and again (until the fusible dissipates) to make additional shapes. A true time-saver! You can save even more time by using a Sulky Iron-on Heat Transfer Pen to transfer your design numerous times onto Totally Stable.

Trace separate pattern pieces of the design onto the right side (non-fusible side) of the Totally Stable. Cut apart into color groups.

To prevent tunneling and puckering when stitching, iron another piece of Totally Stable onto the wrong side of the base fabric on which the appliqué will be applied.

Press the Totally Stable (shiny side down) onto the wrong side of the fabrics. Cut out the patterns on the solid drawn lines.

Remove Totally Stable from fabric pattern pieces. Save for possible reuse. Lightly spray the wrong side of appliqué pieces with KK 2000 on base fabric.

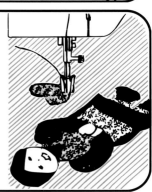

Machine Satin Stitch through all layers, stitching around the cut edges of the fabric pattern pieces. When stitching is completed, tear it away.

Use Totally Stable for Monogramming.

Supports fine fabrics, keeps knits from distorting, and prevents tunneling or puckering.

1. Set up the machine for "Free-Motion".
2. Create the "Letter Grouping" and trace it onto graph paper.
3. Trace the "Letter Grouping" onto Sulky Solvy with a washout marker.
4. Iron Totally Stable onto the wrong side of the fabric to be monogrammed. Place all in the hoop.
5. Monogram. Remove the stabilizers.

**Use Totally Stable to make Stenciled Borders
and Airbrushed Patterns.**

Irons in place keeping sharp edges on the images.

1. Trace the design onto Totally Stable using a permanent-ink, fine-line marker.
2. Cut out the design shape with an Exacto-Knife™.
3. Iron in place on fabric to be stenciled or airbrushed.
4. Stencil or Airbrush. Remove the Totally Stable.

For a repeated re-useable border, fold a length of Totally Stable in a fan fold and cut out the shape on the fold. (It's like making paper dolls.)

Sulky Tear-Easy™

Provides great stability combined with effortless removal that doesn't pull, tear or distort stitches. Professional embroiderers use one, two or three layers of Sulky Tear-Easy to stabilize virtually any fabric. Each layer is then easily torn away separately to prevent the pulling, tearing or distorting of stitches that can occur when tearing away a single layer of a thicker, heavier stabilizer.

Make adorable Angel Embroidered Ornaments, www.sulky.com "Angels" by Joyce Drexler for Great Embroidery.

Available Put-ups in White:
751-01 - 20" x 1 yd. Package
751-03 - 20" x 3 yd. Package
751-08 - 8" x 12 yd. Roll
751-12 - 12" x 12 yd. Roll
751-20 - 20" x 5 yd. Roll
751-25 - 20" x 25 yd. Bolt

Available Put-ups in Black:
752-01 - 20" x 1 yd. Package
752-08 - 8" x 12 yd. Roll
752-12 - 12" x 12 yd. Roll
752-25 - 20" x 25 yd. Bolt

Sulky Stiffy™

Sulky Stiffy is a heavier, denser tear-away stabilizer than Tear-Easy. Try Stiffy when you need extra temporary tear-away backing support for Satin Stitching, Monogramming, Appliquéing and Embroidering, to prevent tunneling, distorting of stitches, and puckering of fabric. Professional Embroiderers use one, two or three layers as a backing to stabilize virtually any fabric.

Available Put-ups:
216-01 - 20" x 1 yd. Package
216-08 - 8" x 11 yd. Roll
216-25 - 20" x 25 yd. Bolt

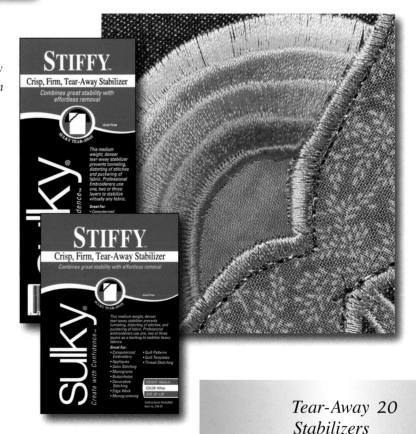

Tear-Away 20
Stabilizers

Sulky Sticky+™
The Self-Adhesive, Tear-Away Stabilizer on a paper-backed release sheet. Ideal for Hooped, Digitized Machine Embroidery.

It's easy to hoop Sulky Sticky+ with the paper side up, the way you would hoop a piece of fabric. Then, using a small sharp knife or straight pin, score the paper and pull it away from the adhesive layer; finger-press your fabric onto the Sticky+. Put the hoop on your sewing machine, and embroider. Or, take the hoop for your embroidery machine and use only the larger outside portion; peel the paper backing off the Sticky+ and stick the adhesive side to the bottom of the outer portion of your hoop. Place your fabric on the hoop and finger-press to adhere. Put the hoop on your sewing machine, and embroider. Small items can be embroidered without basting them to the stabilizer, just finger-press them onto the Sticky+. To make ready-to-wear easier to embroider on areas like cuffs, collars, pockets and socks, just press them onto the Sticky+ and embroider without any additional preparation.

Available Put-ups:
551-01 - 22-1/2" x 1 yd. Package
551-02 - 12 - 7-1/2" x 9" Pre-cut Sheets
551-08 - 7-1/2" x 6 yd. Roll
551-12 - 12" x 6 yd. Roll
551-20 - 21" x 5 yd. Roll
551-25 - 22-1/2" x 25 yd. Bolt

Hoop It. Score It.

Peel Release Sheet Away.

Stick It. Embroider It.

Sulky Totally Stable™
The Iron-On, Tear-Away Stabilizer.

Perfect for knits and stretchy fabrics. Totally stabilizes virtually any fabric in seconds with no time-consuming pinning. Eliminates annoying shifting, sliding and puckering of material. Excess then tears away easily, leaving no sticky residue.

Available Put-ups in White:
661-01 - 20" x 1 yd. Package
661-03 - 20" x 3 yd. Package
661-08 - 8" x 12 yd. Roll
661-12 - 12" x 12 yd. Roll
661-20 - 20" x 5 yd. Roll
661-25 - 20" x 25 yd. Bolt

Available Put-ups in Black:
662-01 - 20" x 1 yd. Package
662-08 - 8" x 12 yd. Roll
662-12 - 12" x 12 yd. Roll
662-25 - 20" x 25 yd. Bolt

*Hot Pants
by Eric Drexler*

Make Magic Windows

Trace a pattern and iron it onto the fabric for a design pattern to follow that won't shift or move.

Make the open windows in which to feature your favorite fabric by first sliding underneath the design area, a feature fabric (right side up) that is slightly larger than the window area. Then, straight stitch over the design and cut out the windows.

Carefully tear away the Totally Stable pattern layer and satin stitch over the straight stitched design. A fun way to decorate a pillow top, vest or jacket.

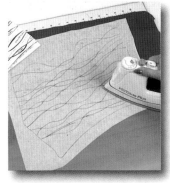

Make the perfect Chevron Quilt Border or table runner using Totally Stable as a foundation. Start with a triangle at the angle you wish to build the border. Sew, flip and iron down each strip. Perfect strip-piecing everytime.

Sulky Heat-Away Clear Film

This clear film is such an improvement over the original mesh-type Heat-Away Stabilizer that resembled muslin. Clear Film allows you to trace designs onto it easily, then place them with the help of Sulky KK 2000 Temporary Spray Adhesive.

What is Heat-Away Clear Film?

You can trace and/or stitch on this medium-weight, clear film. A great alternative to using a water soluble stabilizer when water is not an option for removal.

Use Heat-Away for Cut-Work, Lace-Work, Quilting and more.

Use as a Topper or Stabilizer . . .

on all fabrics that can withstand iron temperatures of 260° - 300° F (120° - 140° C), which is similar to the cotton setting on most irons.

DO NOT USE AN IRONING PRESS. NEVER PRESS WITH STEAM.

Works well on most fabric types. A great alternative to using a cut-away or tear-away stabilizer when you do not want residue left on the fabric, or when tearing could damage the stitching or fabric. Not recommended for high pile fabrics like terry cloth and fleece as it can get trapped in the loops and be difficult to remove.

Use as a Design Template . . .

to trace on, then stitch through, to transfer a design onto fabric when quilting, thread painting, computer embroidering or monogramming.

Place the bumpy side down against the fabric. (Use washout or permanent-ink markers.)

Use as a Disappearing Support Base . . .

to create computer-embroidered lace, battenburg lace, free-motion thread lace, 3-D fabric or thread appliqués and cut-work.

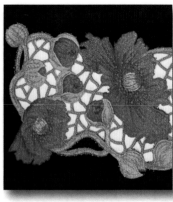

Use Heat-Away Clear Film for Lace-Work and any Open-type Work . . .

- *Trace the lace design onto **Heat-Away Film** using a washout or permanent-ink marker.*
- *Shape, pin and glue lace tape or bias tubing onto **Heat-Away** following the pattern design.*

To "Free-Motion" stitch tape or bias tubes together and needleweave designs inside the tape or bias tubing:

- Thread the top and bobbin with the same color of Sulky 40 wt. Rayon Thread.
- Straight stitch a square over the raw-end areas of the tape, following the outside edges.
- Secure the tape edges where they butt together by stitching them with a free-motion straight stitch.
- Needleweave designs inside the tape loops by first straight stitching along the design lines on the Heat-Away, as called for by the design. In some cases, zig-zag over the straight stitching or form knots by making small circles of straight stitching, or allow a small zig-zag to stitch in place to build up a knot.

Removal is Easy . . .

Once the technique is completed, tear away or cut away as much of the excess film as possible. Preheat your dry iron to 260° - 300° F, or the highest heat setting that the fabric can tolerate. Always test for heat tolerance first on a sample of the fabric being used. Place the iron directly on top of the film and move the iron in a back and forth motion. Iron until all of the film has melted and formed little balls. These particles can then be easily shaken or brushed off.

Tip from Patti Jo Larson: Use a Sticky Lint Roller.

Store . . .

any unused portion in a dry area and protect it from direct sunlight and heat.

Sulky Heat-Away Clear Film

By Nancy Sapin, Freelance National Educator Representing Sulky of America. "When drawing or tracing a pattern onto Heat-Away, I prefer a permanent marker because it won't smear and won't transfer to the fabric. Then, lightly spray KK 2000 onto the bumpy side of the Heat-Away and smooth it onto your project. KK 2000 dissipates quickly with heat, so it's a winning combination. Heat-Away also tears away easily, which removes all large pieces and edge pieces from the project. Anything remaining on your project will just "heat away" like magic, using a DRY iron on a medium cotton setting. It quickly balls up and you just brush it away. Fabulous for a classroom setting when wetting can be difficult. HINT: Draw on the smooth side, and the bumpy side goes against the fabric; and always TEST

Available Put-ups:
850-01 - 19-3/4" x 1 yd. Package
850-08 - 7-7/8" x 9 yd. Roll
850-25 - 19-3/4" x 25 yd. Bolt

New Generation Sulky® KK 2000™

Temporary Spray Adhesive
GOES GREEN

What is KK 2000?

Sulky KK 2000 is the first and only, safe, non-flammable, temporary spray adhesive that uses a low-pressure propellant. It temporarily bonds fabrics and fibers together, virtually eliminating pinning for appliqué, embroidery, quilting, embellishment, stenciling and sewing. Because it contains highly concentrated material and a low pressure propellant, you don't have glue floating all over the room. It is **odorless, colorless, non-toxic and ozone friendly** (no CFC's or HCFC's) with a state-of-the-art spray nozzle that produces a very precise spray pattern that you can direct where you want. No wasteful overspraying, virtually no staining, and it leaves no residue.

When would I use KK 2000?

To enhance the quality and ease of home embroidery, use **KK 2000** to adhere stretchy knits to stabilizers, to adhere Sulky Puffy Foam to fabric, and to adhere any fabric to a hooped stabilizer without hooping the fabric (to eliminate hoop marks). **KK 2000** makes fabrics repositionable for appliqué, for trial fittings of hems, darts, pockets and shoulder pads, and to check the positioning of embellishments like laces, trims, rickrack, yarns, beads and buttons. Use it for quilt basting and to secure tear-away quilt patterns and templates for accurate cutting and stitching.

Where would I use KK 2000?

Sulky KK 2000 was originally developed for appliqué, but it also helps provide drum-tight hooping of stretch fabrics when sprayed onto the Sulky Stabilizer, allowing these fabrics to be placed in their own natural lie. This is particularly useful when dealing with large hoop areas. **KK 2000** also helps stop warping of knit rows during embroidery, and it is great for "unhoopables" such as collars cut on the bias, pocket flaps, etc., as well as mending holes by spraying the damaged area together with a suitable backing before mending.

Why would I use Sulky KK 2000 instead of other brands in the bigger cans?

KK 2000 does not make fabric permanently stiff as other brands can. It completely absorbs into the fibers of the fabric within 24 to 36 hours and disappears within 2-5 days while other spray adhesives can remain stiff and fused many months after application. The convenient, easy-to-hold, smaller can holds just as much glue as the bigger cans - it's the non-flammable, non-toxic, low-pressure propellant that makes the difference.

25

How would I use KK 2000?

- Hold the can 5" to 8" from the receiving surface and spray lightly. Finger-press the underside of the stitching surface onto the tacky surface, and stitch immediately without fear of gumming up the needle.
- One short spray of **KK 2000** is usually equivalent to 2 or more cloud-producing sprays of other brands that use high-pressure, highly flammable, petroleum-based propellants which cause the glue to float out into your room.
- Spray **KK 2000** onto the back of fabric appliqué pieces to hold them securely in place while stitching, yet make them repositionable.
- Spray **KK 2000** onto any and all of the Sulky Stabilizers (except Ultra Solvy) to make a self-stick stabilizer to aid in embroidering difficult-to-hoop items like pockets, edges, buttonhole rows, ribbons, cuffs, collars, socks, neckties, handkerchiefs, doll clothes, etc., as well as for counted cross stitch, silk ribbon work, and hand embroidery in a hoop.
- Spray **KK 2000** on tear-away quilt patterns, templates, or stencils to hold them in place while stitching or stenciling.
- Use **KK 2000** on paper patterns for easy tracing and cutting.
- Always spray away from the sewing machine or machine parts.

What can happen when you use KK 2000 (which is not water soluble) with Solvy or Super Solvy on fleece?

Nancy Cornwell, author of "Adventures with Polar Fleece" and "More Polar Fleece Adventures", advises that to avoid any conflict between the water soluble Solvy (or Super Solvy) and the KK 2000, which is not water soluble, lightly spray the stabilizer NOT the fleece. That way, when you remove the stabilizer, the majority of the KK 2000 goes with the stabilizer, leaving only a trace amount, which disappears over time. Cut away as much of the Solvy or Super Solvy as you can and allow the air to help the KK 2000 absorb into the fibers before you launder. Nancy says, "the more air circulation the better". If you still end up with a gooey residue, Nancy suggests using rubbing alcohol to remove any stickiness. Laundering will not remove it. (Test the rubbing alcohol on a scrap first.)

Visit the Question and Answer Section at
www.sulky.com
24 hours a day for more hints
and troubleshooting tips
on using KK 2000 and all
Sulky products.

Sulky Puffy Foam

What is Sulky Puffy Foam?

Puffy Foam is a high quality Ethylene Vinyl Acetate Film that is made specifically for use on home sewing machines to add flair, 3-dimension and excitement to your designs. It is also used by crafters to stamp on for leather-looking items and for 3-D Shadow Appliqué. It is non-toxic, acid-free, water-resistant and machine washable (machine dry on low) but it is flammable and should not be dry-cleaned. It comes in 12 colors in each of two thicknesses, 2 mm and 3 mm, to create different stitching effects, and there is virtually no waste because even very small pieces can be used. Layers can be stacked to make 4mm and 5mm thicknesses, or whatever will fit under your presser foot or darning foot.

How would I use Puffy Foam?

- Cut a piece of Puffy Foam slightly larger than the design area that you want to "puff"; place it on top of the fabric that is being embroidered, appliquéd, serged or satin stitched so the foam is between the fabric and the thread being applied.

- To embroider over Puffy Foam, hoop the receiving fabric along with the appropriate Sulky Stabilizer backing. Place the Puffy Foam on top of the area to be puffed and hold it in place while you take the first few stitches; or spray Sulky KK 2000 Temporary Spray Adhesive on the foam and finger-press to adhere it in place. Stitch the design, then gently tear away the excess Puffy Foam.

- You may want to stitch over the edges again once the excess Puffy Foam is removed. When Puffy Foam has been torn away from the stitched design, if any little "pokies" remain, shrink them by placing a steam iron very close to them and shoot with steam.

- Use Puffy Foam with computerized or free-motion designs that have satin stitch elements like tapered lettering or tree branches. You can also use it with machine decorative stitches that have satin-stitch elements that will perforate the Puffy Foam, allowing easy removal.

- Use Puffy Foam for crafts. You can stamp it, iron it and distort it for a faux-leather look for embellishments, journals and jewelry.

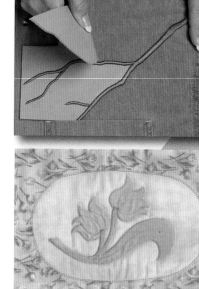

27

Introduction to Recipes for Sewers

Sue Hausmann
*Sewing and
Quilting Edutainer*

"It has been my joy to work with Joyce and Fred Drexler, co-owners of Sulky of America and my good friends for over 25 years. Joyce has been a guest on every series of the America Sews with Sue Hausmann Public Television program since the show began in 1991. While our time together began professionally, it quickly grew into a close friendship with Joyce and Fred. We love to share grandchildren stories, travel escapades and "sew" much more.

I began sewing for myself in 4-H when I was 10 and have been sewing ever since. In teaching and training, and thanks to the Public Television Program, America Sews with Sue Hausmann, it has been my privilege to share the joy of sewing with people all over the world. However, my greatest compliment came over the Christmas holiday as I was shortening jeans and my granddaughter Sage, age 4, sat on my lap at the sewing machine and said "Grandma, you are the best sewer in the world!"

In my early days it was my joy to teach Beginning Sewing in the Adult Education Program at a local Community College and at a High School, where one week of class was devoted to the sewing supplies and the structure of garments and projects. For many years, I experimented with different types and brands of interfacings and elements to give garments and home dec the right "structure", hand, and hang. In the 70's, I began to embellish with appliqué and decorative stitches and I learned to embroider free motion from one of Joyce's Speed Stitch

Kits. Even then, Joyce and Fred were influencing my life and the lives of "sew" many sewers. Who would have believed where this all took us!

This time of embellishment was my first introduction to stabilizers. It was actually very strange to me to buy this package of non-woven fiber that you would not leave in your garment or craft. At first, it seemed like a waste of money to buy a stabilizer, stitch through it, then tear it away. It only took one project to convince me that using a stabilizer was worth it! The finished project was proof that quality Sulky Stabilizers really made a difference! The fabric was "stabilized" well while embellishing and, once removed, the fabric was not stiff! Plus, these non-woven stabilizers did not dull my sewing machine needle or damage my machine. I was teaching "machine arts" at the time and Sulky Stabilizers became a part of our class supply list.

That was just the beginning and because the types of Sulky Stabilizers were limited, we needed to select embellishment techniques with care for specialty fabrics. Over the next 20+ years, Sulky has continued to develop, test, and introduce quality stabilizer products so that now we can embellish and embroider virtually any design or technique on virtually any fabric type or weight!

I love to sew garments and as my stabilizer supply grew, I found myself experimenting with different stabilizers for sewing techniques. My stabilizer holder (see page 185) keeps them at my fingertips, and many of the Sulky Stabilizers are even better than what I was using for these techniques when sewing in the past. I've outlined a few of my favorite uses for Sulky Stabilizers for sewing on the next pages." --- Sue

28

Make Patterns

Recipe for Success

Presented by: Sue Hausmann

Stabilizer:
- Sulky Soft 'n Sheer™ - permanent
- Sulky KK 2000™ Temporary Spray Adhesive

Procedure:
Use Sulky Soft 'n Sheer to create very lightweight, sturdy, permanent, reuseable patterns and save the flimsy tissue patterns as masters.

- Use yardage from a bolt of Sulky Soft 'n Sheer.
- Cut pieces of Soft 'n Sheer a little larger than the pattern pieces you wish to trace.
- Lightly spray the Soft 'n Sheer with KK 2000 and smooth the pattern piece over it. The KK 2000 keeps the pattern in place while you trace it.
- Write all notations on the Soft 'n Sheer pattern pieces.
- Store in zip-lock baggies along with the original pattern package.

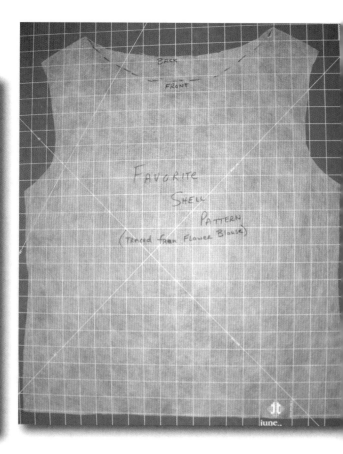

Make Alterations

Recipe for Success

Presented by: Sue Hausmann

Stabilizer:
- Sulky Totally Stable™ - iron-on, temporary

Procedure:
Use Sulky Totally Stable to make alterations to patterns.

- Cut the pattern as needed, then insert a piece of Totally Stable and fuse it in place to add length or to make a designer detail adjustment.
- Because you can iron Totally Stable then pull it off, reposition it, and press it again many times, you can experiment with the pattern details before cutting into the fabric.

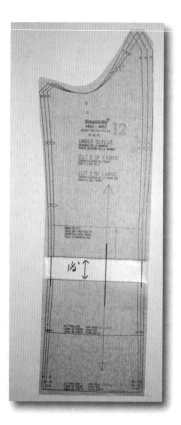

Decorative Inserts

Recipe for Success

Stabilizer:

- Sulky Cut-Away Plus™ - permanent

Procedure:

Use Sulky Cut-Away Plus to create a stable foundation for specialty-made fabric embellishments when adding them to a garment.

- Use yardage from a bolt of Sulky Cut-Away Plus.
- Lay the completed "bubbly" shirred fabric on a similar size piece of Cut-Away Plus and baste the shirred fabric to it.
- The Cut-Away Plus stabilizes the bumpy, textured piece, giving you a firmer, more manageable piece to work with.
- Do not try to stretch your shirred piece flat. On the back of the Cut-Away Plus, mark the width that you want the finished shirred piece to be; serge, or use an overcast stitch, on this line.
- Sew your shirred piece into your garment or appliquéd area. Cut away the Cut-Away Plus.

Complete instructions on how to make Diane's "Fiber Bubbles" are in the book "Quick and Easy Weekend Quilting with Sulky". Visit Diane's website to read the incredible story of the creation of her Bernina Fashion Show Garment: www.designonawhim.com

Presented by:
Diane Gloystein
Designer and Freelance
National Educator
Representing Sulky of America

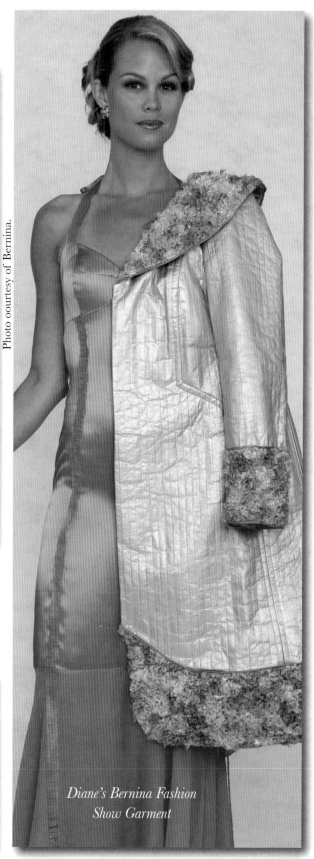

Photo oourtesy of Bernina.

Diane's Bernina Fashion Show Garment

30

Recipe for Success

Presented by:
Nancy Estep
National Free-lance
Sewing Educator

Stabilizers:
- Sulky Fuse 'n Stitch™ - iron-on, permanent
- Sulky Tender Touch™ - iron-on, permanent

Procedure:
Tote: "Sunday Dinner Apron", a Vanilla House Design. "Frenchy Bags" designed by Amy Butler featuring Moda fabrics.

- Fuse 'n Stitch was used to stiffen the Apron's waistband, and Tender Touch was used to add body to the neck strap and apron ties.

- To add the stiffness you need, iron Sulky Fuse 'n-Stitch onto the wrong side of the fabric.

- You will be able to topstitch and/or decorative stitch easily because Fuse 'n Stitch stabilizes the fabric, and remains on the fabric to keep it stiff.

- When you make **Tote Bags and Purses** and you want the sides and handles to be sturdy, simply fuse Sulky Fuse 'n Stitch to the wrong side of your fabric.

- Fuse 'n Stitch is perfect for **Costumes** when you need "stiffness" as in special hats, cuffs, wings, tails, etc., and for **Belts** where you want to retain shape.

Facings

Recipe for Success

Stabilizer:
- Sulky Tender Touch™ - iron-on, permanent

Procedure:

I have used Tender Touch as my "facing fabric" to eliminate bulk and still have the ability to fuse the facing to the wrong side of the garment so it stays in place.

- This is great for "fast facing" on costumes and other quick garments and when a garment fabric is too heavy to use as a facing.
- Cut the facing pieces from Sulky Tender Touch.
- Sew them to the garment piece in the same way you would stitch a facing, with the fusible side out.
- Trim your seam allowances with pinking shears to eliminate bulk. Turn the facing to the wrong side and fuse in place.
- One of the first places I used this technique was on a metal sequin evening fabric that had "points" in the pattern of the sequins. I made the hem edge of the top beautiful by placing a strip of Sulky Tender Touch, right sides together with the sequin fabric along the bottom edge of the sequin top; then I stitched along the shape of the "points", trimmed the excess seam allowance along the points, turned the Tender Touch to the wrong side and fused it in place. Tender Touch "facings" finish the neck edge and sleeve hems.

Underlining

Recipe for Success

Stabilizer:
- Sulky Tender Touch™ - iron-on, permanent

Procedure:

I keep a bolt of Tender Touch on hand so I have the wider widths available for underlining some fabrics.

- Since underlining will change the "hand" of the fabric, when a fabric tends to be too lightweight for the type of garment I am making, I fuse Tender Touch to the wrong side of the entire piece of fabric before cutting out the garment pieces. I have a lightweight tweed wool and silk jacket that would have "sagged and bagged" as I wore it if I had not added the Tender Touch underlining.

Presented by: Sue Hausmann

Make a Hem Gauge

Recipe for Success

Stabilizer:
- Sulky Cut-Away Plus™ - permanent

Procedure:

Use Sulky Cut-Away Plus to create a Hem Gauge.

- Cut a rectangle 4" wide by 12" long for skirts and 4" x 6" for pants; use a permanent marking pen to draw lines across the 12" and 6" length at ½", 1", 1½", 1¾", 2", 2½" and 3" from the edge.
- By inserting my "Hem Gauge" into the hem I can fold the hem allowance up over the Cut-Away Plus to the correct line and press it there.
- You can make a Sulky Cut-Away Plus "Hem Gauge" for any size hem you need. This can be really helpful for home dec sewing when you need a double 4" hem in your drapes. For a curved hem on skirts, etc., use the original curve of the skirt as your pattern to cut the Sulky Cut-Away Plus piece, then measure from the curve for your hem allowance and mark.

Tame Seams & Edges

Recipe for Success

Stabilizer:
- Sulky Tear-Easy™ - temporary tear-away

Procedure:

I tame construction seams on the most challenging fabrics with Sulky Tear-Easy.

- Some lightweight, or sheer, or slippery fabrics can be difficult to stitch (even the seams) without puckering or slipping.
- Simply place strips of Sulky Tear-Easy under the fabric, right sides together, as you sew.
- Then, tear away the stabilizer when the stitching is complete.

Presented by: Sue Hausmann

Stay-stitching

Recipe for Success

Stabilizer:
- Sulky Tender Touch™ - iron-on, permanent

Procedure:

I love to cut strips of Tender Touch with the length of the strip on the least stretchy direction to "interface" the seam allowances where stretch can occur while sewing.

- This is especially important when putting a zipper into the seam of a bias cut skirt. Simply "interface" the seam allowances in the zipper area with strips of Sulky Tender Touch.

Interface Knits

Recipe for Success

Stabilizer:
- Sulky Tender Touch™ - iron-on, permanent

Procedure:

For years, I've been a real fan of fusible tricot interfacing and I was "sew" happy when Sulky introduced Tender Touch since the packages and rolls are very easy to work with and to store. Tender Touch fusible tricot is the interfacing in most of the garments I sew today.

- Sulky Tender Touch has more stretch in one direction than in the other, so keep the stretchier direction on the crosswise of your pattern pieces.
- When pinning the facing pattern piece to cut the interfacing, pin inside the seamlines, then slip your pinking shear under the pattern piece and cut along the seamline to eliminate the bulk in the seams.
- Using the pinking shears means the edge of the interfacing won't "press through" as a ridge on your garment.
- To fuse your Tender Touch interface piece to the garment piece, place the garment piece, wrong side up, on your ironing surface, and place the Tender Touch interfacing piece, fusible side down, with the pinked edges at the seamlines.
- Before fusing together, give the pieces a "blast of steam" to remove any wrinkles or shrinkage. Place a Sulky Tear-Easy "press cloth" on top and press the Tender Touch onto the fabric with lots of steam. Do not move the iron back and forth! Hold the iron in one place for 10 seconds and then move to the next place.
- Turn the fabric over and use another "press cloth" to press from the right side. Mark one of your Sulky Tear-Easy "press cloths" to be used for fusible only.
- Replace "press cloths" often.

> **Tip:** *I usually interface the garment not the facing because I want the structure on the garment side. There are exceptions such as sheers, lightweight silks, very light t-shirt knits, etc., because the "fusible dots" can show through on the right side on very light, sheer fabrics. In this case, press the Tender Touch onto the facing piece or use Sulky Cut-Away Soft 'n Sheer as a "sew-in" interfacing.*

Add Decorative Details

Recipe for Success

Presented by: Sue Hausmann

Stabilizers:
- Sulky Tear-Easy™ - temporary tear-away
- Sulky Stiffy™ - temporary tear-away
- Sulky Super Solvy™ - water soluble
- Sulky Fabri-Solvy™ - fabric-like water soluble

Procedure:

In most cases for decorative stitching, I use two layers of Sulky Tear-Easy Stabilizer (stack the two pieces in opposite directions for best stabilizing and easiest tearing away) or one layer of Sulky Stiffy. If you will see your project from both sides or you feel you need a stabilizer on top due to a napped fabric, etc., use Sulky Super Solvy or Fabri-Solvy as a topper since they are water soluble and will wash away after stitching.

- Use Sulky Stabilizers to add perfect Decorative Details. Using a Sulky Stabilizer for decorative details should be a given, yet many times we forget this simple step.
- Any time you are decorative stitching on any weight of fabric, be sure to put a Sulky Stabilizer under your area to be stitched to support the fabric and also serve as a smooth layer to feed along the feed dogs/teeth of your machine.
- Sometimes a texture on the underside of the fabric can "hang up" the stitching as you sew. It is key to let your sewing machine feed dogs/teeth do the feeding of the fabric.
- Many people wonder why they have "distorted" decorative stitching. This is usually due to "helping the fabric" by pulling it through the sewing machine. When stitching, it is your job to only guide the fabric, not feed it through. If your machine needs help feeding the fabric, have it serviced or think about getting a new machine!

Buttonholes

Recipe for Success

Presented by:
Ellen Osten
Sulky National Director
of Education

Stabilizer:
- Sulky Solvy™ Liquid - water soluble

Procedure:

It's a good idea to always keep some liquid Solvy mixture on hand. It is the ideal solution for stabilizing the area to be stitched for a buttonhole.

- Formula for making liquid Solvy:
  1 - 20" x 36" piece of Solvy per 8 oz. of water; or
  1 - 18" x 20" piece of Super Solvy per 8 oz. of water; or
  1 - 9" x 20" piece of Ultra Solvy per 8 oz. of water.
- Simply brush it on the area. Let dry.
- Stitch the perfectly stabilized buttonhole.
- Rinse out.

Add to Ready-to-Wear

Recipe for Success

Presented by: Sue Hausmann

Stabilizer:

• Sulky Totally Stable™ - iron-on, temporary

Procedure:

Create the Perfect Pattern for adding Designer Fabric details to Ready-to-Wear Garments with Sulky Totally Stable. Joyce showed this technique on America Sews and I have used it many times.

• You can create a perfect pattern from which to cut a piece of fabric to then stitch onto the specific area of a garment as a designer detail.

• For example, to add a print, batik or strip-quilted fabric yoke over the yoke of a jean jacket or to add a print cuff detail, place the "slick" side of Sulky Totally Stable on the garment over the area to be "detailed" and press until the seamlines or edges of the garment area to be "covered" with your designer detail fabric are pressed into the Totally Stable.

• Pull the Totally Stable off the garment and place it on a flat surface. Add seam allowances along the edges of the "yoke" or " cuff", then cut out the new "pattern" you have created.

• You may need to create a right and a left yoke pattern, etc. Place the slick side of your Totally Stable pattern down onto the designer fabric, press to fuse in place, and cut out the piece. (As long as you keep the slick side down when you create the pattern and when you cut the fabric, your designer fabric piece will be in the "right direction".)

• To put the designer detail fabric onto your garment, pull off the Sulky Totally Stable pattern and fuse a ½" strip of paper-backed Steam-a-Seam (fusible web) on the right side on the seam allowances. Leave the paper in place and press the seam allowances to the wrong side. Remove the paper and fuse the designer fabric piece to the garment for perfect, one-of-a-kind designer detail.

Cut-work

Recipe for Success

Presented by:
Ellen Osten
Sulky National Director
of Education

Thread:

• Sulky 40 wt. Rayon

Stabilizer:

• Sulky Heat-Away Clear Film - iron-away, or you can use Sulky Super Solvy - water soluble

Design & Procedure:

This cut-work design is available under "Patterns" on the CD in the back of this book.

• Cut out the jacket fabric pieces using your favorite jacket pattern.
• Trace the cut-work design onto the Super Solvy or Heat-Away using a fine-line, permanent-ink marker.
• Place the traced design over the front piece of the jacket according to the design pattern placement guide.
• Straight stitch three times, following the design lines.
• Carefully cut away the fabric only where indicated.
• Satin Stitch over the straight stitching using a 2mm width.
• Remove the Super Solvy or Heat-Away following the directions on page 12 or 24.

Manipulated Fabrics

Recipe for Success

Presented by: *Carol Ingram*

Stabilizer:
- Sulky Tender Touch™ - iron-on, permanent

Procedure:
- These pillows incorporate a scrunching/pleating technique. In order to make the fabric manipulation permanent, iron Sulky Tender Touch onto the back of the prepared fabric.
- Tender Touch was perfect for this Silk Dupioni Fabric. It didn't change the "hand" of the fabric when ironed on.

Sue Hausmann, on the left, and Carol Ingram on the T.V. show, ***"America Sews with Sue Hausmann"***.

Hand Embroidery

Recipe for Success

Presented by: *Carol Ingram*

Hand Thread:
- Sulky 12 wt. or 30 wt. Solid Color Cotton
- Sulky 12 wt. or 30 wt. Cotton Blendables®

Stabilizers:
- Sulky Tender Touch™ - iron-on, permanent
- Sulky Soft 'n Sheer™ - cut-away, permanent
- Sulky KK 2000™ Temporary Spray Adhesive

Procedure:
- To prevent show-through and to add body to a pillow top or framed piece when hand stitching, iron Tender Touch onto the back of the fabric, or spray the fabric with Sulky KK 2000 and smooth Soft 'n Sheer onto the wrong side of the fabric being worked.

It's always best to have your pillow top or framed work lined with Tender Touch or Soft 'n Sheer to prevent the show through of pulled threads when hand embroidering.

Recipe for Success

Stabilizers:
- Sulky Fuse 'n Stitch™ - iron-on, permanent
- Sulky Tear-Easy™ - tear-away, temporary
- Sulky Tender Touch™ - iron-on, permanent

Procedure:
- Place two fat quarters, right sides together, and trim to 17" long x 22" wide. If your fabric is directional, *keep in mind that the 22" is the width*.
- Keep both pieces together and fold in half, with the 17" measurement on the fold.
- To round the corners, place a round object (like a large bowl) in the lower corner. Trace the shape and cut on the line.
- For the waistband, cut two 5" strips from one of the waist-band fabrics. Remove the selvage edges. Cut one strip in half across the narrow width and sew one half to each end of the long strip. Repeat with the other waistband fabric.
- Place Sulky Tear-Easy underneath the apron fabric where the appliqués are going to be applied to help your stitches be nice and smooth without creeping or tunneling.
- Follow manufacturer's instructions to apply the appliqués to the apron skirt fabrics using a fusible web.
- Use a Sulky Cotton Blendables® Thread color that coordinates with the colors in your fabrics to blanket-stitch around the design. Carefully remove the Tear-Easy from the back of the design areas.
- Place the apron pieces, right sides together, and stitch the curved edge. Leave the top straight edge unstitched. Clip the seam allowance in the curved areas every 1/2", almost to the stitching, so that the curves lay flat. Turn right sides out and press.
- Measure the top width of the apron. It should be 20". Mark the center. Set aside.
- On the waistband fabrics, mark the center of each piece. From the center, measure 10" in both directions and make a mark at each spot. (Adjust this measurement if your apron top is more or less than 20".) This is the apron placement.
- Cut a piece of Sulky Fuse 'n Stitch 4-1/2" x 20"; center it on one of the waistbands and press it in place to add body to the fabric.
- Cut two pieces of Tender Touch 4-1/2" wide x the length of each tie. Fuse in place on the wrong side of one set of the ties (the same side on which the Fuse 'n Stitch is fused).
- Place the two long waistband pieces, right sides together, Trim the ends at 45° angles. Stitch all four sides, leaving open between the marks.
- Turn the waist band and press well, using a point turner in the corners and ends.
- Insert the apron into the open side of the waistband. Pin in place, being careful that both the front and back edges are even. Use Sulky Blendables Thread to straight stitch (top-stitch) in place around all edges of the waistband and ties, about 1/8" away from edge.
- Topstitch the apron.

Presented by:
Bonnie Forkner
Editor/Founder

www.goinghometoroost.com

This is Bonnie's original Reversible Apron Design. The Bird and Deer Appliqué Designs are on the CD in the back of this book.

Fabrics:
- 2 coordinating fat quarters for apron fronts or 1/2 yard of each
- 1/3 yard each of two coordinating fabrics for apron waist band and ties *
- * For the apron and deer appliqué, Bonnie used Amy Butler's fabric line, "Love" by Rowan Fabrics. For the bird appliqué, she used Joel Dewberry's "Woodgrain" by Westminster Fibers.

Optional Appliqué Method:
For hand-stitching an appliqué with a needle-turned look, use Sulky Fabri-Solvy:

- *Trace the design onto the Sulky Fabri-Solvy.*
- *Place right sides together with the appliqué fabric.*
- *Sew on the traced line.*
- *Slit the Fabri-Solvy in the center and turn the design right side out.*
- *Press well with an iron (no steam) and use a point turner to aid turning in sharp corners.*

A Reversible
Appliquéd Apron

Monogrammed Bolster

by Carol Ingram

Finished Size: 19" x 21"

Materials

- 5/8 yd. Silk Dupioni - Gold
- 12" x 44" Silk Dupioni - Contrasting Rust
- 1 - 20" x 22" Poly Fleece
- Sulky Tear-Easy™ Stabilizer
- Sulky Tender Touch™ Stabilizer
- Sulky KK 2000™ Temporary Spray Adhesive
- Sulky 40 wt. Rayon Embroidery Thread -
   #1021 Maple, #1243 Spring Moss,
   #630 Moss Green
- 2 spools of Sulky 30 wt. Rayon #1021 Maple
- Heavy-duty, Needle-nosed Pliers
- Sulky Polyester Clear Invisible Thread

- Digitized Monogram Design *(from the*
   Sulky Embroidery Design Club Collection)
- 44" of 1/4" Cotton Cord for Cording/Piping
- 23" heavy String or Ribbon for gathering ends
- Zipper or Cording/Piping Foot • Chalk Marker
- Twin Needle - 4.5/90
- Long Plastic Ruler and a 6" clear Quilters Square
- 1 - Prim Dritz Covered Button kit – size #100 - 2-1/2"
   plus 7" x 14" Gold Silk Dupioni and two 7" x 14" Tear-Easy
- Floral Wire - 20 to 24 gauge - 1/4 lb. - 38" long
- 1 Low-loft, Queen-size, Polyester Quilt Batt
- General Sewing Supplies

Preparation and Construction:

1. Fuse Sulky Tender Touch onto the back of the entire 5/8 yd. of Gold Silk Dupioni and cut a 20" x 22" piece from it.

2. Tautly hoop two layers of Sulky Tear-Easy (layered in opposite directions). Spray Sulky KK 2000 on the top layer, then finger-press the center of the 20" x 22" Silk Dupioni (Tender Touch side down) over the Tear-Easy. Slide the hoop onto your machine and embroider the monogram design in the center.

3. Unhoop and tear away the excess Tear-Easy, one layer at a time. Place the fabric, design side down, and press the design.

4. Place a 6" square Quilter's Ruler over the embroidery and use a chalk marker to draw a line all the way around the square to create a framed border.

5. To mark the twin needle stitching lines, use a 24" ruler and a chalk marker to draw diagonal lines 1-1/2" apart from the upper left corner all across the silk top (but not over the 6" square in the center) to the lower right corner.

6. Spray KK 2000 on a 20" x 22" piece of Tear-Easy; smooth a 20" x 22" layer of poly fleece over it. Spray KK 2000 on the back of the embroidered silk dupioni and smooth it over the poly fleece.

7. Insert a 4.5/90 twin needle. Thread the top from 2 spools of Sulky 30 wt. Rayon #1021 Maple. Slowly wind the bobbin with Sulky Clear Polyester Invisible Thread. Use a 3.0 to 3.5 length straight stitch to stitch across all of the chalk lines except the two short 6" lines at the top and bottom of the embroidery square. First, stitch across all of the diagonal lines, then do the two short lines that complete the 6" square.

8. Insert a single 12/80 embroidery needle. Thread the top with Sulky 40 wt. Rayon either #630 Moss Green or #1243 Spring Moss. Select your favorite decorative stitch and stitch it down the center of the diagonal rows created by the twin needle stitching.

Prepare Piping and Casing:

1. Make 44" of piping using cotton cording and the same gold color Silk Dupioni used for the pillow.

2. Stitch the piping onto both ends of the prepared pillow top, (the 22" edges).

3. Cut two 5" x 22" pieces of contrasting rust Silk Dupioni. To make a casing on one long side of each piece (to later insert a ribbon for gathering the ends of the bolster), fold over 1/4" and press (wrong sides together) the 22" length of one piece; then fold over again, this time 1-1/4", and press. Repeat for one long edge of the second piece.

4. Lay the raw edge, right sides together, over the piping on one end of the prepared pillow; stitch in place. (The pillow is still flat.) Do the same on the opposite end.

5. To create the tubular pillow, fold the pillow top lengthwise, right sides together, with the ends laid flat outward (opening up the pressed edges); use a 1/2" seam allowance to straight stitch the seam. Fold the seam ends back in and press. (We pressed the casing before the long seam was sewn because it was easier to press in these folds when the piece was laying flat.) Now, you just need to use the tip of your iron to touch up the seamed and previously-pressed areas.

5. Straight stitch along this edge to secure it, then straight stitch 1/4" down from the top of the folded edge to create the casing for the drawstring.

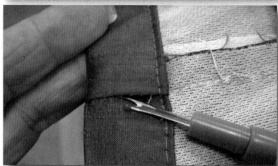

6. Use a seam ripper to remove several stitches in the seam at both casing ends.

7. Tie about 2 feet of yarn (or a ribbon) on a large safety pin and feed it through the casing at one end. Repeat at the other end. Set aside for now.

Make the Covered Buttons:

1. Spray KK 2000 on one 7" x 14" piece of Tear-Easy. Layer a second 7" x 14" piece of Tear-Easy on top of it and spray KK 2000 on it; smooth a 7" x 14" piece of gold Silk Dupioni over it.

2. Use a 24" ruler and a chalk marker to mark the stitching lines on the diagonal all across the 7" x 14" piece, every 1/2" or 3/4".

3. Thread the top with the same color of Sulky 40 wt. Rayon that you used in #8 on the previous page, and use the same decorative stitch to stitch over all the diagonal lines.

4. Following the package directions for the 2-1/2" covered button kit, cut a circular pattern from the cardboard. Lay it over the decoratively-stitched fabric and mark around it with a chalk marker. Repeat.

5. Cut two circles from the fabric and cover two buttons as per manufacturer's directions.

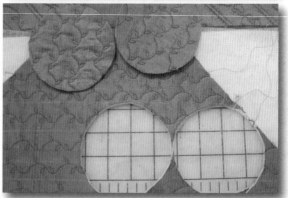

Finish Making the Bolster:

There are several ways to stuff this bolster, such as with loose batting or a purchased, foam-shaped filling. But Carol wanted her buttons to stay tight to the ends and create a slight dimple in the gathering on the ends, so she used a queen-size, low-loft quilt batt to finish hers as follows:

1. Remove the batt from the plastic sleeve and carefully unroll it, keeping it in its shape; cut approximately 10" from one of the folded ends (save the 10" for some future use).
2. Lay a 38" length of floral wire (20-24 gauge) down the center of the roll with the wire protruding several inches from both ends; re-roll the batt to its original form.
3. Secure the roll with a couple of lightweight rubber bands to hold it in place while you push it into the length of the bolster. Once the batt is inside, clip the rubber bands and make sure the wire is still protruding from each end.
4. Pull the yarn/ribbon drawstring at each end to gather the ends of the bolster; secure them tightly (the wire should still be protruding from the gathered ends).
5. Secure one button on one end of the wire by twisting a small J-shaped piece at the end of the wire, and attaching it to the button shank on the back. Close the "J" on the wire to secure the button.

6. Grasp the wire on the other end of the pillow and pull it tightly to snug the two buttons. Use a heavy-duty, needle-nosed pliers to cut the wire about two to three inches shorter than the length of the pillow and attach it (using the "J" method above in #5) to the button shank on the second button on the opposite end. You want the "pull" created by the shortening of the wire to look similar to the picture below left.

Be sure to check out the exciting Sulky Embroidery Design Club.

Visit: www.sulky.com

Featured Designers:
Carol Ingram and Joyce Drexler

42

Knitted Designer Pillows

Look at all the fun you can have! Cut up an old sweater or shawl or knit your own mitered-square using designer yarns to make these awesome pillows.

Materials for Rectangular Pillow

- 3/4 yd. of Silk Dupioni
- 2-1/2 yds. of 1/2" Cotton Cording
- 2 - 17-1/2" squares of Fleece Batting
- Bag of Polyfil™
- Sulky Tender Touch™ and Sulky Tear-Easy™ Stabilizers
- Sulky Polyester Clear Invisible Thread
- Sulky KK 2000™ Temporary Spray Adhesive
- 12/80 or 14/90 Topstitch Needle
- Steam Iron and Press Cloth

- Zipper Foot, Yarn Couching Foot and Yarn Feeder Guides (an Open-Toe Applique Foot could also be used), Button Placement Foot and a Cording Foot
- Yarn and Knitting Needles (select needle size to suit chosen yarn) or a 9" x 17" piece cut from an old sweater or shawl
- Gridded, padded board or ironing board
- Yarn for Couching
- Various Buttons
- General Sewing Supplies

Knit or use a Recycled Sweater

1. Knit a 9" x 17" rectangle or, to use a recycled sweater or shawl, cut a 9" x 17" piece from it. *Before cutting, keep it from unraveling by placing and fusing a 1" wide strip of Sulky Tender Touch over the center of the cutting lines, then cut down the center of the Tender Touch strips on the line (which you can see through the Tender Touch).*

2. Pin the finished knitted or cut rectangle on a gridded ironing surface so that it measures 9" x 17". Place a damp press cloth over it and, with a dry iron, press until dry.

3. Lay a 10" x 18" piece of Sulky Tender Touch on the underside of the blocked knitted piece, cover with a press cloth and fuse them together.

4. Fuse Tender Touch onto the wrong side of the entire 3/4 yd. of Silk Dupioni.

5. From the stabilized Silk Dupioni, cut two 17-1/2" squares.

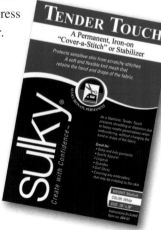

by Carol Ingram

Featuring Sulky® Tear-Easy™ and Tender Touch™ Stabilizers.

*These hand-knitted pillows add a lot of texture to any decor. The
teal rectanglar pillow features an Entrelac pattern. For knitting
instructions Google: entrelac knitting. The knitted Mitered-Square
is applied to a pillow foundation fabric. For Mitered-Square
knitting instructions and videos, Google: mitered knitted
square. Some pillows have additional embellishments
added by couching more yarn on the remaining portion of the pillow.*

44

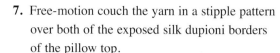

6. Use the remaining silk and the 1/2" cord to make enough piping to trim completely around the outside edge of a finished 17" pillow, plus 2", and an extra 17-1/2" piece of piping for the front.

7. Cut two 18" squares of Sulky Tear-Easy Stabilizer. *The 20" Roll of Tear-Easy is ideal for pillows.* Set aside.

Create the Pillow Top:

1. Set aside one 17-1/2" silk square to be used for the pillow back.

2. Spray Sulky KK 2000 Temporary Spray Adhesive on the back of the prepared 9" x 17" knitted rectangle and lay it on one edge of the 17-1/2" silk square to be used for the pillow top.

3. Cut two 18" squares of Tear-Easy and spray KK 2000 on both sides of them, then apply them, one at a time, to the back of the 17-1/2" pillow top.

4. Thread the top and bobbin with Sulky Clear Polyester Invisible Thread. **Wind the bobbin slowly, and only about 1/2 full.** Insert a 12/80 or 14/90 topstitch needle.

5. Lay the prepared 17-1/2" piping down the center of the pillow, just under the edge of the knitted 9" x 17" rectangle. Butt the knitting far enough up to the piping to cover the raw edges; pin it in place. Use a zipper foot to stitch it in place close to the piping, while stitching it to the pillow top.

6. Set up the machine for free-motion straight stitching. Attach the yarn couching foot, yarn feeder guides, and the extra ball of yarn; thread the yarn into the foot.

7. Free-motion couch the yarn in a stipple pattern over both of the exposed silk dupioni borders of the pillow top.

   Hint: If you do not have a yarn couching foot to couch down the yarn, use an open-toe appliqué foot with a machine-fed, small, zig-zag stitch.

8. Attach the button placement foot and sew on as many buttons as desired, scattering them around the yarn couching to create a pleasing affect.

Editor's Note:

Silk is an exotic fabric that sometimes can react to chemicals differently than other fabrics do, which is why we **spray the stabilized (Tender Touch) side of the Silk Dupioni with Sulky KK 2000 when we can, and not the silk itself.** *Although we have used KK-2000 many times directly on silk without any staining, we do occasionally hear of this happening.*

So, be sure to test EVERY piece of silk that you use. This is much less likely to happen when using the new and improved KK 2000 (with a green cap) which has a new, state-of-the-art spray nozzle which delivers a more precise spray pattern, and allows you to hold the can closer (5" to 8") when you spray.

If staining should occur on silk or another exotic fabric, it will almost always come out. **See the "Question and Answer Section" at www.sulky.com, for more details.**

Construct the Pillow:

1. Spray KK 2000 onto the wrong side of the front piece of Silk Dupioni and the wrong side of the front of the pillow; smooth a 17-1/2" square of fleece batting over each sprayed piece.

2. Finish the pillow by sewing piping all around the edges, leaving an opening to stuff it with Polyfil. Turn and sew the opening closed by hand.

3. If you need instructions on how to make piping, you will find them on the CD in the back of this book.

Another Pillow Option:

Knitted, Mitered-Square Pillows:

These pillows are constructed in the same manner as the rectangular pillow (just smaller), and the knitted square is placed in the middle of the silk pillow top, or on a corner with two silk borders showing.

Use a quilter's square ruler and chalk marker to trace around the square for placement. Leave an appropriate, attractive margin of 2" to 4" beyond the edges of the square which can be decorative-stitched or otherwise embellished as desired.

The Pink/Black/White pillow on page 44 was knitted with size 8 needles and rayon and eyelash yarn held together as one, using the Mitered-Square technique.

Eyelash yarn will hang over the edges, making a pretty, feathered edge.

For Mitered-Square knitting instructions and videos, google: mitered knitted square.

Taming Fabrics

Complete instructions for the pillows shown below are on the CD in the back of this book.

Carol Ingram, on the right, with Pokey Bolton, host of the PBS TV show, **"Quilting Arts"** featuring Sulky® KK 2000™, Sulky Tear-Easy™ and Sulky Tender Touch™ Stabilizers.

by Carol Ingram

Introduction to Recipes for Crafters

by Carol Ingram
Artist and Designer
for Sulky of America

"With five girls and two boys, I have spent a great deal of time in the last 50+ years at the sewing machine, and doing arts and crafts with my children and grandchildren.

'Sew' many of those years were spent sewing prom dresses, Halloween costumes, bridal dresses and beauty pageant dresses, not to mention the endless clothing alterations and repairs. I have also done my share of volunteer work at the various schools including sewing for cheerleaders, band, and soccer, decorating class rooms and parade floats, and teaching art.

Apparently, early on, I developed a reputation, and my children's immediate response to the call for volunteers was, 'My mom will do it'. So, I got to spend many enjoyable years with my children doing creative things.

Since being 'on-call' is over in that sense, I have found new joy in creating in other areas of my life, such as textile arts and crafts, which began in earnest with my association with Sulky of America in 1995, when I won the Grand Prize in the 'Everyone Loves Sulky Challenge'. I needed an artistic outlet, and they wanted new talent and ideas. And it has been quite a ride since then! I have made really good friends at Sulky of America, and we continue to share a love of sewing, embroidery, fiber art and crafts.

'Crafting', as defined by the dictionary, is a 'skill involving a practical application of art for the making of decorative items by hand'. Creating unique craft items requires an idea, a desire to create, and the proper tools and products.

I believe that what a person creates has more value when it is a personal expression of their own ideas. Given the right equipment and knowledge, most crafts are simple to do, and are truly a devoted declaration of love, more valuable than any purchased item, whether it is a hand-dyed, hand-made quilt, or a crafted bowl or bookmark.

Through my many years of association with Sulky, I have had the privilege of using their quality products, paired with my artistic ability, training and years of sewing experience, and it has turned into a successful and very rewarding hobby (and sometimes, job).

I find a great deal of pleasure and contentment in my retirement years, just being in my studio, creating new and exciting things to share both in the Sulky books and on Sulky-sponsored PBS television shows. Fortunately, someone (friend or family) usually likes what I create, and then I have a gift to give as an expression of my love, too.

How well these sewing and crafting techniques turn out is the result of fearless experimentation, practice, and individual artistic expression. Sulky knew I enjoyed the challenge of working with new products, and soon found that while experimenting, I would take their products to many new extremes. Just say,. 'You can't do that with Puffy Foam', and I'd say 'Why not?!'; and figure out how to do it!

Nothing is more fun for me than taking a product that is intended for one thing, and creating a whole new use (or abuse) for it. I have considered it a challenge using Sulky products to help bridge the gap between the sewing and crafting fields. With my love for both art and sewing, good things have happened. I hope you enjoy trying the fruits of my efforts." ...Carol

Sulky Iron-On Transfer Pens

What are Sulky Iron-On, Transfer Pens?

Sulky permanent, non-bleeding Transfer Pens come in 8 colors and white. The colored ones store the ink in a well inside the pen until activated by pumping the point, then writing or drawing with them. The sublimation ink inside the eight colors is specially made to transfer multiple times (we've gotten up to 20 great transfers from one inking). Results will vary depending on how long the dry iron is left on the transfer each time, and whether the user has preheated the area to be transferred onto, as well as the ironing surface.

How would I use them?

You can trace or draw anything on regular copier, printer or notebook paper. You can transfer that image onto any surface that can withstand the heat of an iron. Always do a test first on a sample of the receiving surface to assure precise results. When transferring onto any surface where ink penetration might occur, protect the surface underneath. When transferring a design that won't be covered with embellishments, the receiving fabric must contain at least 35% polyester to insure the permanency of the ink; wait 3-5 days before laundering gently with mild detergent. When outlining patterns for numbers and letters that you want to transfer, reverse the image.

Look for sets of pens like those pictured or individually blister-packaged.

49

Carol Ingram created this beautiful Sulky Iron-on Transfer Leaf Sweatshirt by tracing the outline of different real leaves onto vellum. She made pools of transfer ink on the waxy side of Totally Stable to create a palette. She then applied the transfer ink to the inside of the outlined leaves using a small paint brush and Q-tips. The shading turned out fantastic! After transferring the leaf designs onto the sweatshirt with a hot iron, Carol used fabric markers to enhance them. The fabric facing, interfaced with Sulky Tender Touch Iron-on Stabilizer, was added for additional color.

Stenciled Wall Panel

Recipe for Success

Thread & Needle:
- Sulky 12 wt, and 30 wt. Cotton
- Size 16/100 Needle

Stabilizers:
- Sulky Cut-Away Plus™ - permanent, dyeable
- Sulky Fuse 'n Stitch™ - iron-on, permanent
- Sulky KK 2000™ Temporary Spray Adhesive

Procedure:
To make this adorable wall panel, Natalie Albritton stenciled on Sulky Dyed Cut-Away Plus.
- Print out the Parrot found on the CD - enlarge as desired on a copier.
- Spray the pattern with Sulky KK 2000 and place it under clear stencil plastic to temporarily secure it in place while you trace it with a Sharpie™ , extra-fine, permanent-ink marker.
- Lay the stencil pattern over a piece of glass and use a stencil-cutting knife to cut out the tree branch, parrot and several leaf designs.
- Spray KK 2000 onto the back of the chosen stencils and place them on an 18" x 24" piece of dyed Cut-Away Plus.
- Arrange the Parrot and leaves per photo on the right. Stencil the entire pattern as desired using stencil brushes and your favorite Oil Pastels. Once dry, set the paint by ironing over it with a muslin cloth.
- Iron an 18" x 24" piece of Sulky Fuse 'n Stitch onto one side of an 18" x 24" piece of fleece.
- Spray KK 2000 onto the back of the stenciled Cut-Away Plus design and secure it to the other side of the prepared fleece.
- Thread the top with Sulky 12 wt. Cotton and put a matching 30 wt. Cotton in the bobbin. Stitch around the outside of the stenciled design with either a free-motion or machine-fed straight stitch. Embellish as desired.
- Using a zig-zag blade in a rotary cutter, trim your finished piece to measure 15-1/2" x 18".
- Place strips of double-sided mounting tape on all sides and down the center back, and secure it to a black mounting board that is 1" bigger all around than the stenciled panel.
- Secure a black braided cord or ribbon to the upper section of the panel using a 2" strip of black duct tape over the ends of the cord or ribbon.

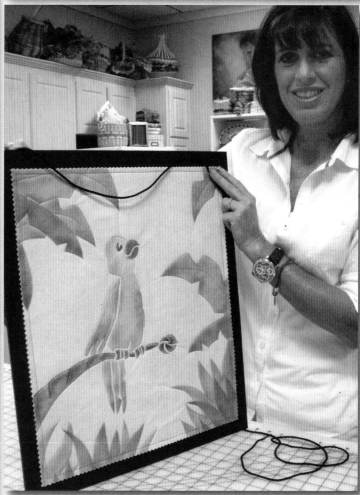

by Natalie Albritton, Carol Ingram's daughter, in Carol's Florida studio.

50

Recipe for Success

Thread:
- Sulky 40 wt. Rayon Thread

Stabilizer:
- Sulky Soft 'n Sheer™ - permanent, cut-away
- Sulky KK 2000™ Temporary Spray Adhesive

Procedure:

"Little Louie" is from Carol Ingram's Snow Family Cactus Punch Embroidery Card #22. www.sulky.com

- Hoop one layer of Sulky Soft 'n Sheer in your machine embroidery hoop.
- Cut a piece of White Sulky 2 mm Puffy Foam larger than the design area; spray Sulky KK 2000 on one side and place it in the center of the hoop.
- Mirror image the designs and embroider them.
- Remove from the hoop and pull the Puffy Foam away from the design.

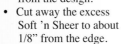

- Cut away the excess Soft 'n Sheer to about 1/8" from the edge.
- If there is any Puffy Foam poking through the design, shrink the little "pokies" away by holding a steam iron about 1" above the design and steam.

- Melt away any remaining Soft 'n Sheer with a wood-burning tool.
- Cut a 20" piece of rat-tail cord; fold it in half and make a loop.
- Tie an overhand knot 3" down from the top of the loop.
- Lay the cord down the the center and glue it in place.
- Lay a small wad of batting between the two mirror-imaged snow-men, sandwiching the cord and batting inside.
- Slide one or two 4mm plastic beads on the bottom end of the cords. Glue them in place.

51

Recipe for Success

Stabilizer:
• Sulky Sticky+ - temporary, tear-away

Procedure:

When you want to color your next thread sketch with crayons, put Sulky Sticky+ on the back of the fabric first to keep it from getting distorted, stretched or crinkled during the coloring process. Makes it a lot more fun! And problem free! Fun for all ages.

• Trace a design onto your background fabric.
• Adhere Sulky Sticky+ on the wrong side of your background fabric to support and stabilize the fabric so it doesn't shift or crinkle while you color.
• **Important: Remove Sticky+ within a few hours of application or it may become difficult to remove.**
• To get a smooth texture, put a piece of fleece or batting under the fabric while you color.
• To create different textures, try coloring with the fabric over sandpaper or screening.
• When coloring, Cindee likes to use the side of her crayon to give a softer, more blended effect.
• Once the crayon is applied on the fabric, it can be difficult to remove, but you can use other colors to lighten or darken your original color.

by Cindee Kaufman
Grand Junction, CO

This beautiful crayon wreath project can be found in the book: **Sulky Secrets to Successful Embroidery.**

Recipe for Success

Thread & Needle:
- Sulky 12 wt. Cotton Solid Colors and Blendables®
- Cameo Punch Needle

Stabilizer and Pens:
- Sulky Tender Touch™ - iron-on, permanent
- Sulky Iron-On Transfer Pens

Procedure:

"This was a purchased Punch-It Design by Lizzie Kate, 'A Little Lamb', #pi003 (www.lizziekate.com). I substituted Sulky Solid Color and Blendables® Cotton Threads for the floss recommended in the pattern. The result was quite spectacular even though I am a complete novice at this. Enough so, that I gave this as a gift to Joyce Drexler, author of this book and my best friend!"

- Make a photocopy of your design, then use a brown or black Sulky Iron-On Transfer Pen to trace over the outlines of the design. Since there are 8 colors available, you can fill in areas with the appropriate colors and really speed up your work.
- Iron the colored transfer onto your Weaver's Cloth using a dry iron at a cotton setting. You hardly need to glance back to the original pattern once you have your colors transferred.
- It's important to use a quality, non-slip hoop to hold your work tautly and maintain the original design shape. Punch from the "wrong side" where your transfer is brightest.
- Always hold your needle perpendicular to the fabric at a 90° angle.
- **It was such a joy not to have to separate floss and re-thread all the time. I put the Sulky spool on a spool holder and used just one strand of it continuously for the entire color area, without once cutting my thread and re-threading!** *Wow! Punchneedle has just become streamlined!*
- When your design is complete, lay it, thread side down, on a terry cloth towel, and iron a piece of Sulky Tender Touch (slightly larger than the design area) over it to help secure the stitches.
- Frame, make a small pin-cushion, or work into a pillow, purse, quilted piece or garment as desired.

by Patti Lee
Editor, Designer and Sulky Vice-President, Consumer Relations

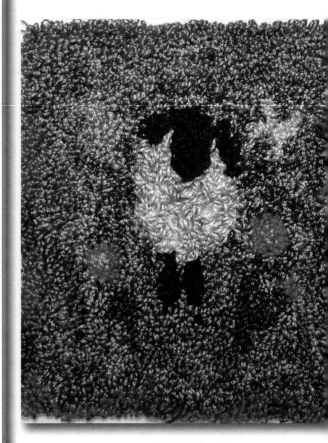

"A Little Lamb"

53

Above: Guy and Noelle Taylor. Below: Eric Drexler Photo Pin-Weaving.

Recipe for Success

Project by: Carol Ingram, Artist and Designer

Thread
- Sulky 12 wt. Solid or Blendables® Cotton Thread

Stabilizer:
- Sulky Fuse 'n Stitch - iron-on, permanent

Procedure:
- Transfer a photo to fabric. Iron Fuse 'n Stitch to the back.
- Cut the prepared photo fabric in PRECISE horizontal 1/4" strips; stop about 1/8" away from details you wish to emphasize. When you begin weaving, you will adjust these areas. DO NOT CUT THROUGH THE LEFT VERTICAL EDGE OF THE PHOTO FABRIC.
- Cut another piece of Fuse 'n Stitch 1/2" larger than fabric.
- Pin it to a pressing pad, with the fusible side up.
- Place pins at a slight angle every 1/4" horizontally across the top and bottom of the board.
- Use Sulky 12 wt. Cotton Thread and tie a knot onto the bottom left corner pin.
- String the thread tautly up to and across the top left corner pin from right to left, then back down to and under the same bottom pin from left to right (making it double), continuing over to and around the right side of the next bottom pin, then up to and around the second top pin. Continue stringing down, over, up, down, over, etc. until all rows are strung. Then knot the thread on the last pin.
- Lay the pre-cut photo fabric over the Fuse 'n Stitch and strung thread. Use a straight-edged, sharp-pointed scissors to cut apart the first horizontal strip at the left margin. With tweezers, start in the center around the face and weave the strip between the threads to the left and right of the face. Lift the strip away from the threads and cut apart each succeeding strip at the margin, one at a time, and weave it between the threads, keeping each strip snug up against the previously woven strip; leave no open spaces. Pin in place. Check to be sure everything is straight.
- Cover the photo area with a non-stick pressing sheet. Use a steam iron at a cotton setting to press and fuse the threads and strips of photo fabric to the Fuse 'n Stitch.
- Remove the pins and press once again from the reverse side.
- Square up and sew the framing fabric strips around the finished piece as desired. Press. Iron a larger piece of Fuse 'n Stitch on the wrong side of the piece with borders.
- Bind or frame as desired.

From the book, "An Updated Supplement to Sulky's Secrets to Successful Stabilizing" #900B-17.

cherish The

inner child

by Carol Ingram

Featuring Sulky Liquid Solvy, Sticky+,
Fuse 'n Stitch, Cut-Away Plus and Stiffy Stabilizers

*Carol's "Cherish the Inner Child"
wall art piece is a multi-media mixture
meshed together to create a piece
of art that, at first, you might be reluctant
to attempt because you have little or no
art training or artistic ability.*

*But Carol will show you just how easy
it really is. All of the images were
traced, then applied to the background.
As long as you have an outline picture
for inspiration and lettering to trace,
this is a very doable project.*

Carol Ingram, on the left
with Sue Hausmann taping the
PBS TV show
***"America Sews with Sue
Hausmann"***.

*Carol also did this
smaller wallhanging
in a different color-way.
She embellished it with
Dyed Cut-Away Plus
flowers, embroidered
thread-lace leaves,
quilting, and finally,
beading to give it an
added twinkle effect.*

56

Materials:

Design Patterns can be found on the CD in the back of this book

- Cut-Away Plus™ Stabilizer
- Fuse 'n Stitch™ Stabilizer
- Solvy™ or Super Solvy™ Stabilizer
- Totally Stable™ Stabilizer
- Sulky 12 wt. and 30 wt. Cotton Blendables® Thread
- Sulky Invisible Thread
- Sulky KK 2000™ Temporary Spray Adhesive
- Sulky Iron-on Transfer Pens
- Water   • Margarita Salt
- Inks and Sponge Tip Applicators
- Paintstik™ Oil Paint Sticks
- Stencil Brushes   • Fabric Pens
- Jacquard™ Fabric Dyes
- Tsukineko™ Inks
- Beads and Beading Needle
- A non-stick surface, i.e, either a plastic tablecloth, non-stick pressing sheet or wax paper
- June Tailor™ Quilter's Cut & Press
- Clear, Open-Toe Foot
- Size 14/90 Topstitch Needle
- Light Table
- Warm & Natural™ Cotton Batting
- Rotary Cutter & Mat
- General Sewing Supplies

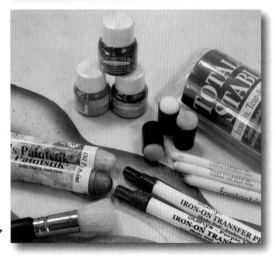

Create the beautiful background by hand dying the Cut-Away Plus Stabilizer.

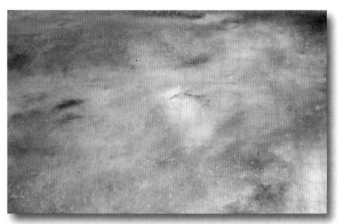

The first step is to create the beautiful background "fabric" which is actually stabilizer that looks like art fabric once you have prepared it with paints and/or dyes. This is really fun and easy. Start with a large piece of Sulky Cut-Away Plus Stabilizer, which comes in a folded package, rolls or bolts. While you can iron Cut-Away Plus, it is best for this project to use a piece that has not been folded. For the larger size wall art, the bolts work well. (Carol dyes yards at a time, then cuts them to the size she needs for her projects.) We used a liquid fabric dye (Jacquard or Pebeo) to create the background in this project. (Bolts of all Sulky Stabilizers can be ordered through your local retailer or on-line at www.speedstitch.com or www.bostonthread.com)

1. Cut a piece of Cut-Away Plus 8" to 10" larger than the desired finished measurement; wet it thoroughly and lay it on a table that is covered with a plastic cloth. Use paper towels to wipe the excess water from around the Cut-Away Plus. Let it lay flat until it is just slightly damp through and through.

2. Mix various colors of dyes, some thicker than others, in plastic containers. This is strictly your own judgement call as the artist. Brush your dye mixtures onto the damp Cut-Away Plus piece. Create the color scheme that best suits your decor. Let it dry thoroughly.

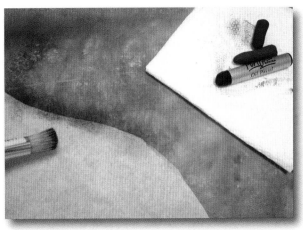

3. Using a stamp that you have inked with fabric dye, stamp around the outer edges of the dry piece. The images don't have to be perfect. Having some partial images of the leaves adds interest.

5. Scrub the tip of a stencil brush over an oil or water-based pastel stick to collect paint on the tip of the brush. Then wipe the excess onto a paper towel, leaving just a light remnant of paint for subtle color.

Brush with a circular motion to pull the paint along one edge of the ironed-on, Totally Stable, wave pattern. Carol chose to shade the wave darkly along one edge, while leaving it lighter in between.

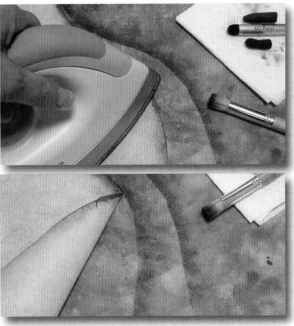

4. To make the patterns for the long wavy lines, use a rotary cutter to cut long wavy pieces of Sulky Totally Stable.

Place the wavy-shaped Totally Stable, slick side down, diagonally onto the background starting in the upper left corner about 1" from the top. Iron in place.

6. Remove your wave pattern and reposition it again, aligning it along the first line radiating out from the starting point; continue to stencil to achieve your desired effect. Totally Stable can be peeled up, repositioned and ironed many times.

7. Add different colored stenciled lines to use both sides of your Totally Stable pattern.

The child's face and the words and lettering were traced and transferred using Sulky Iron-on Transfer Pens. The shading was done using Tsukineko Inks with a Fantastix™ applicator tip.

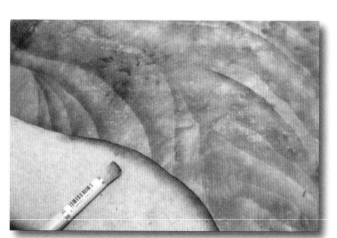

8. Make as many wavy lines as you desire.

Create the Face & Lettering using
Sulky Iron-on Transfer Pens:

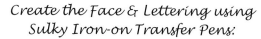

1. You can use your computer to create the words and print them out. When using Sulky Iron-On Transfer Pens, you must trace the letters in reverse, and this is very easy when you use a light box.

2. Place the printed lettering upside down and trace the design onto paper with the color of Sulky Iron-on Transfer Pen that you would like to have on your art piece. The letters will be backwards as you trace them so they will be right-side-up when you transfer them onto your art piece.

3. Sulky Transfer pen tracings can be used to transfer the words multiple times (as many as 8-10 before re-inking) if the ironing surface and the receiving surface are preheated prior to applying the transfer pattern each time.

4. Lightly spray KK 2000 on the transfer-ink side of the paper and place it, ink side down, on your art piece. You should be looking at your original tracing of the word, right side up.

5. Cover the paper with a press cloth and press with a **dry iron** set to the high setting. Since movement may smudge the ink, hold the iron still for 5-7 seconds; do not move or slide the iron, lift and press only. Before removing the transfer paper, lift up one edge and check to see if it has transferred to your satisfaction. If not, continue pressing and rechecking.

When using Sulky Iron-On Transfer Pens on fabric, the fabric should be at least 35% polyester for the ink transfer color to be the most vibrant and maintain its permanency. Because Sulky Cut-Away Plus is 90% polyester, it will permanently accept the transfer inks, paint and dyes.

6. You can enhance the transferred image by using fabric pens.

Prepare for Quilting:

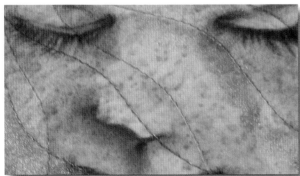

1. Trim the art piece to the desired framing size, with an additional 2 inches added all around if you intend to stretch it over stretcher bars.

2. Cut the batting and backing fabric the same size.

3. Layer for quilting:
   A. Place the backing fabric, wrong side up, on the table. Lightly spray the wrong side with Sulky KK 2000 Temporary Spray Adhesive.
   B. Smooth the batting over the sprayed side of the backing fabric.
   C. Lightly spray the wrong side of the art piece with KK 2000. Finger-press the sticky side over the batting and make sure that all layers are laying smoothly.

Set up the Machine for Quilting:

1. Insert a new 14/90 top-stitch needle. Thread the top with Sulky 12 wt. or 30 wt. Cotton Blendables Thread in a complementary color.

2. Wind Sulky Polyester Invisible Thread on the bobbin.
   Carol prefers Sulky Polyester Invisible Thread in the bobbin because it helps her avoid changing bobbins during the many multi-color thread changes on some projects. She also suggests winding the bobbin at slow speed and only half full. Invisible Thread is so fine, you will get much more on a half-full bobbin than a bobbin filled with regular thread.

3. Select the straight stitch with a 4.0 length.

4. Attach a clear, open-toe foot.

5. Slightly loosen the top tension, if needed, for a balanced stitch.

6. Select the needle down position, if available.

Quilt It:

Quilt your art piece on the wavy lines, adding the quilting effect as desired. (When quilting a large piece, Carol likes to use the even-feed foot.)

Further Embellish It:

1. Dye more Cut-Away Plus in degrees of intensity in colors that will complement the art piece. Fan fold the dry Cut-Away Plus and cut out various sizes of flowers. Because Cut-Away Plus is non-woven, it will not fray, so there is no need for further finishing of the edges.

2. From the same piece of Cut-Away Plus, cut out leaves in slightly different sizes. Sandwich the leaves in a hoop between two layers of Sulky Solvy Stabilizer.

3. Thread the top with Sulky 30 wt. Cotton Blendables in a green to match your dyed leaves; straight stitch over the leaves, embellishing them with as much thread as desired.

4. Layer the flowers and leaves, and tack them in place with Sulky Polyester Invisible Thread as you sew on beads over the top of them. Scrunch the leaves so they ripple before tacking them in place.

Finishing It:

1. Decide how you wish to display your Art Piece.

2. Possibilities:
    A. Bind the edges like a traditional quilt.
    B. Stretch the piece on stretcher bars.
    C. Frame the piece.

Another beautiful Southwest Scene by Carol Ingram using similar techniques.

Unique Ultra Suede Scarves

by Eric Drexler

National Sulky Educator
Inspired by Diane Gloystein's Waterfall Scarf - see page 70.

*Everybody loves Ultra Suede®, and adding some luscious Sulky® Rayons,
Sulky Blendables® or Sulky Holoshimmer™ Metallic Threads to them will have heads
turning your way. Making this type of scarf is a lot of fun because it is so easy.
With the help of Sulky Ultra Solvy™ you can create a one-of-a-kind original in
an afternoon once your Ultra Suede designs are cut out.
Using these techniques will have everyone asking. . .
"How did you do that?"*

Pokey Bolton on the left,
and Eric Drexler
as seen on the PBS
TV Show -
"Quilting Arts".

Featuring:
* *Sulky Ultra Solvy Stabilizer*
* *Sulky Rayon Threads*
* *Sulky Blendables Threads*
* *Sulky Holoshimmer Metallic Threads*

*Eric's display of Ultra Suede
Scarves simply takes your
breath away. Each one
expresses a different interest
and feeling. It is Eric's hope
that his scarves will inspire you
to create a scarf theme that best
expresses your special interests.
See closeups on page 69.*

62

Materials:

- Sulky Ultra Solvy Stabilizer the desired length and width (add 3"- 4" to the desired finished length to allow for shrinkage). *Ultra Solvy comes in various lengths and widths. If you calculate it right you can get several scarves out of one size roll.*
- 10" x 12" piece of Ultra Suede (makes 1 long, skinny scarf)
- Matching colors of Sulky 12 wt. and 30 wt. Cotton Blendables
- Vertical spool pin if using Sulky Holoshimmer or Sulky Sliver™ Metallic Thread
- Size 14/90 – 16/100 Topstitch, Embroidery, or Metallic needle
- General Purpose or Stretch-Stitch Presser Foot, Optional Spring-loaded Free-Motion, Darning or Embroidery Foot
- 1 – 2 Empty Bobbins
- Fine-line, Permanent-Ink Marker
- Sulky Black or Brown Iron-On Transfer Pen, Plain Paper and a Dry Iron **Check out the Iron-On Transfer Pen video at www.sulky.com**
- Rotary Cutting mat with grid lines
- Rotary Cutter and Quilter's Ruler
- Small, sharp, pointed Scissors
- Scotch® Magic Tape
- Q-Tips™
- Small bowl of water
- 1 paper towel
- **Use your computer's printer to print out the heart designs found on the CD in the back of this book.**
- General Sewing Supplies

Other heart scarf or belt ideas.

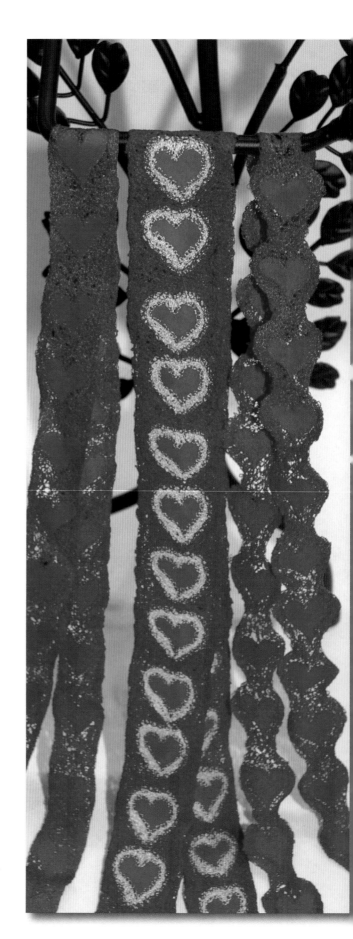

1. Use a black or brown Sulky Iron-on Transfer Pen (see page 49 for more info) to draw or trace onto plain paper the multiple heart designs found on the CD in the back of this book. Since you are going to *cut away all of the pen lines,* make sure the inside measurement of the heart is the size you want the finished design to be.

   Set a dry iron on a cotton setting. Preheat the ironing surface as well as the Ultra Suede (from the wrong side) by pressing them quickly.

2. Lightly spray Sulky KK 2000 Temporary Spray Adhesive onto the design side of the paper to help keep it from moving while pressing.

   Place the paper image, ink side down, onto the right side of the Ultra Suede. To get multiple transfers of the images, press each one quickly with a dry iron (do not slide the iron). Before moving the iron and the paper image, check to see if it has transferred as desired by lifting only an edge of the paper.

3. When satisfied, remove the paper image and place it, ink side down again, in an open area; repeat the transferring process. Since you only need a light image to cut out, you can repeat this up to 10-12 times or more without re-inking.

   Once you have transferred the image as many times as needed to produce the number of hearts you want, cut them out, making sure the edges are evenly cut to achieve a nice smooth edge to the hearts.

4. Cut a strip of Ultra Solvy slightly larger than the length and width you want your finished scarf to be. Twenty-inch rolls make a nice shawl size or cut it in half for 10" wide scarves.

5. **Pin or tape the Ultra Solvy flat onto a gridded mat or ironing board cover.** Lay the hearts on the Ultra Solvy in the desired design format. Eric wanted his to be symmetrical so he followed the inch grid measurements to keep the spacing uniform. *(Since the scarf will move and sway when worn, it is not critical that the design elements be perfectly spaced, but it should be close.* Dip a Q-tip into a small bowl of water and dab it on a paper towel to soak up the excess. Lift up a heart and lightly moisten the wrong side of it. Place it back on the Ultra Solvy (the moisture will cause it to stick). Repeat for all of the other hearts.

64

Stitching down the Ultra Suede Hearts:

Set up your Machine:

Option 1 - Machine-Fed:

Makes a light, hand-tatting effect when the Ultra Solvy is washed out.

- Insert a new 14/90 or 16/100 Topstitch, Metallic, Embroidery, or Denim Needle
- Wind onto 2 Bobbins, either Sulky 30 wt. or 12 wt. (if your machine will handle 12 wt.) Blendables Multi-colored Cotton Thread, and put one in the machine
- Thread the top with a matching weight Sulky 30 wt. or 12 wt. Cotton Thread *(whichever weight works best in your machine)*
- Select the Triple-Straight-Stitch (two stitches forward and one back)
- Select a 2.5mm Stitch Length
- Select Needle-Down option, if available
- Attach an All-Purpose or Stretch Stitch Presser Foot

Option 2 - Free-Motion

Creates a lacy effect when Ultra Solvy is washed out.

- Insert a new 14/90 or 16/100 Topstitch, Metallic, Embroidery, or Denim Needle
- Thread the top with a coordinating Sulky 30 wt. Variegated Rayon Thread
- Wind 2 Bobbins with the same thread and put one in the machine
- Select the Stipple Stitch
- Select Needle-Down option, if available
- Cover or drop the Feed Teeth
- Lower the top tension slightly
- Attach a Free-Motion Foot
- A hoop will not be needed

65

Option 1 - Machine-Fed - Triple-Straight-Stitch

For this scarf, Eric used Sulky 12 wt. Cotton Blendables as the upper thread and a matching Sulky 30 wt. Cotton Blendables in the Bobbin. He used the triple-straight-stitch that takes two stitches forward and one back.

1. Start in the top left corner and stitch straight down the horizontal long side, through the center of each Ultra Suede heart.

2. When you reach the end, stop with your needle down in the middle of the last Ultra Suede heart in that row. Turn 90° and stitch to the center of the next heart; turn 90° more and stitch back up through the center of the remaining hearts, to the end of that row.

3. Repeat until all of the long, horizontal rows are sewn. You may need to overlap some of the stitches to get to the center of an Ultra Suede heart to start stitching the short vertical rows.

4. Repeat the previous steps for the short vertical rows. When sewing these short rows, you may find it easier to work in small 8" areas. To do this, roll the Ultra Solvy as you go, then slightly wet a small spot (on the top) by the edge to make it stick to the rest of the rolled-up piece and hold it all in place.

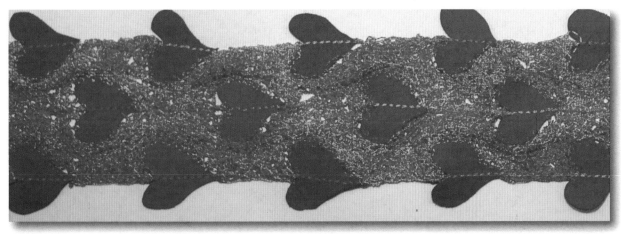

Another scarf idea. A combination of Option 1 & 2.

To create the lace look, it is not necessary to hoop your fabric since Ultra Solvy is a very firm foundation stabilizer on which your hearts are adhered so they won't move, shift, or pucker.

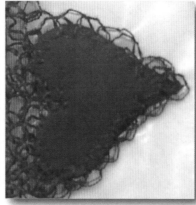

1. Begin by stitching tiny stippling stitches in a circular fashion around the outside of each Ultra Suede heart. Stitch predominantly on the Ultra Solvy, but also over all outer edges of the heart to avoid having holes when the Ultra Solvy is dissolved.

2. After all of the hearts are outlined and secured with the tiny stipple stitching, continue to free-motion stitch little circles in the open areas, always connecting to the outlined heart shapes.

3. Make sure all of the circles are overlapping. Check how densely it is filled in while the project is out of the machine. Inspect it by holding it up to the light.

   Mark the "thin" areas with a straight pin for easy identification when you go back to the machine to fill them in more.

4. Actual fabric can be created by filling in heavily, or you can create a dainty, lacy look if the stitches are spread out more. Just make sure they all overlap or there will be holes after the Ultra Solvy is washed out.

   The beauty of this project is that you get to practice your free-motion technique and any mistakes you may have made will be covered by other stitches. (Eric practices right on the scarf by writing his name, by making small and large circles, by stitching continuous-line quilting and cross-over quilting stitches; then he simply stitches over all of it with more circles.) For longer wearability, go around the outside edge one more time to make sure it is heavier.

Remove the Ultra Solvy Stabilizer:

- Because Ultra Solvy is the most dense of all of the Solvys, it takes a volume of water and more agitation to wash it away.
- Fill a top-loading washer with warm water.
- Place the scarf in a lingerie bag or discarded pantyhose and put it into the washer. (Do not add any other clothing or detergent to the water at this time.)
- Run the wash cycle for a few minutes until the scarf is thoroughly agitated and the Ultra Solvy has been entirely removed from the scarf. If it still feels sticky when removed, then it needs to be put back in the washer and agitated longer.
- Line dry, and lightly press if needed.
  If your stitches are dense, it might take more agitation to completely rinse out all of the Ultra Solvy.
- In order to not waste the water, once the Ultra Solvy is thoroughly rinsed out of the scarf, you can then add detergent and a load of clothes, and run the full wash cycle. The dissolved Ultra Solvy will not harm your clothes, washer or septic system.
- If you find you have any large holes in your scarf, iron it flat after it dries, then lightly spritz it with water and adhere another piece of Ultra Solvy on the wrong side, a few inches larger all around than the hole.
- When it dries, it is ready for you to add more fill stitches to hide any holes. You can speed up the drying process by using a hand-held hair dryer.

> **TIP:** *If you want a larger piece of Ultra Solvy to make a shawl or vest, you can easily attach two pieces together by moistening the top of one piece and the bottom of another. Smooth the moistened edges together and let dry for a permanent bond.*
>
> *This technique can be used to attach a variety of fabrics to Ultra Solvy by simply dipping them in water, blotting out the excess water, and applying them to the Ultra Solvy. Since Ultra Suede is essentially waterproof, Eric moistened the Ultra Solvy and applied the fabric to the wetted surface.*

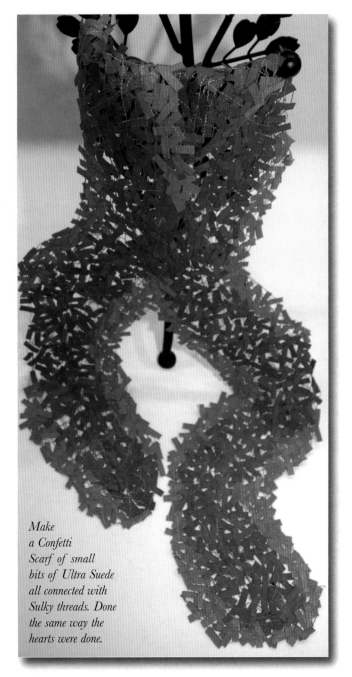

Make a Confetti Scarf of small bits of Ultra Suede all connected with Sulky threads. Done the same way the hearts were done.

Instead of hearts, try simple squares and Blendables® Threads.

68

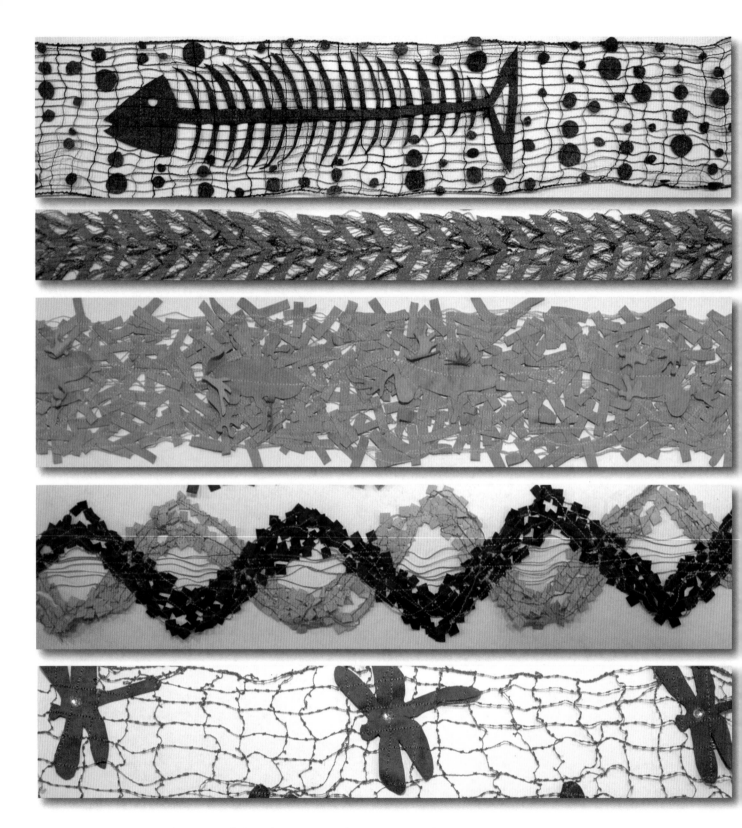

More beautiful Ultra Suede Scarves by Eric. Do you see the frogs?

The dragonfly scarf was made by June Garris. All of the various designs used on the scarves shown are available on the CD found in the back of this book.

Waterfall Scarf

Complete instructions for the scarf shown below are on the CD in the back of this book.

by Diane Gloystein

Bonus Project

Embroidered Trivets & More

Your friends and family will wonder "How did you do that?" as they examine the reversible trivet that you made just for them. Learn Nancy's technique to make a center square that showcases embroidery or theme fabric and incorporates the fabric-wrapped clothesline technique used in making bowls. Nancy will also share how she creates square coasters and coaster holders, square bowls, breadbaskets, wallhangings, photo frames and purses, all using this same center-focal-point technique.

Joyce Drexler, on the left, with Pokey Bolton on the PBS TV set, taping **"QUILTING ARTS"**, Series 400.

Recipe: How to make a **thick** water soluble solution from one of the Sulky Solvy Stabilizers - by Pam Laba

Recipe: *Dissolve whichever Sulky Solvy you have on hand; Pam prefers Super Solvy.*

3 yards Solvy™	to 1 cup of water
1-1/4 yards Super Solvy™	to 1 cup of water
5/8 yard Ultra Solvy™	to 1 cup of water

Directions:

• Heat one cup of water in the microwave for about 30 seconds so it will be warm to the touch. Warm water aids in dissolving the Solvy faster.

• In quarter-yard increments, add either Solvy, Super Solvy or Ultra Solvy to the water in the amounts listed above, stirring each increment until dissolved.

• If needed through the dissolving process, reheat the solution in the microwave for 10 seconds or so.

by Nancy Sapin

Designer and Freelance National Educator
Representing Sulky of America

Featuring Sulky® Super Solvy™
and Fuse 'n Stitch™ Stabilizers

Look for Joyce's Sulky
Designer Rayon
Thread Collection ---
"Preferred Greens"
at your local fabric
or quilt shop.

It is the perfect
companion to Joyce's
"Jumbo Ferns"
Embroidery Card by
GreatEmbroideryDesigns.com.
visit: www.sulky.com and
check out the new Sulky
Embroidery Design Club.

Materials:

For all of the coordinated, embroidered, corded crafts.

- **Jumbo Fabulous Ferns Embroidery Card #3020GNP** - (www.sulky.com)

  by Joyce Drexler for GreatEmbroideryDesigns.com. Designs used: #26342 Small Boston Fern and #26334 Large Boston Fern **or substitute theme fabric in place of embroidery**

- Sewing Machine with Embroidery capabilities plus:
  - 5" x 7" or larger hoop capacity
  - Closed-toe (for flat surfaces) & Open-toe (for curved surfaces like baskets) Appliqué or Zig-zag Feet
  - Jeans-a-Ma-Jig™ to level presser foot
  - 14/90 Topstitch Needle and 16/100 Denim Needle
- Sulky 40 wt. Rayon Threads for Embroidering Ferns: #1177 Avocado, #630 Moss Green, #1104 Pastel Yellow-Green, #1173 Med. Army Green, #1005 Black
- Sulky Super Solvy - 1-1/4 yds. to make liquid Solvy
- Sulky Ultra Solvy - 2 layers for each embroidery
- Sulky Fuse 'n Stitch Permanent Stabilizer - 8" Roll
- Sulky 30 wt. Cotton Blendables® Thread #4019 Forest Floor
- Sulky Clear Invisible Polyester Thread
- Sulky White Polyester Bobbin Thread
- Sulky KK 2000™ Temporary Spray Adhesive
- Lt. Green Fabric on which to embroider Ferns - cut to fit hoop:

  For Small Fern - 9" x 12"; Large Fern - 10-1/2" x 18"
- Approximately 1/4 yd. coordinating Fabric per Trivet
- Steam-A-Seam2™ Fusible Web with a release sheet
- 2 or 3 Hinged Clothespins or Quilter's Straight Pins
- Q-Tips™ and Spray Bottle of Water
- Acid-Free Glue Stick
- Foam Paint Brush & Water Container
- Stiletto or Bamboo Skewer
- Sharp Shears and Thread Scissors
- Jumbo (60mm) Blade Rotary Cutter, Mat and Ruler
- Mini-Iron (optional) and a Steam Iron & Pressing Surface
- Wellington™ medium-load, multi-purpose braided cotton clothesline with a synthetic core, 7/32" #81842. K-Mart® sells this product and Ace® Hardware clothesline is comparable. It can also be purchased on-line through various sources, but not all other cotton clothesline products will give the best results. See individual project photos for amounts needed.

▲ **Trivet with a 5-1/2" Center**

- 7/32" Clothesline Cord - 35 feet
- 1/2 yd. Light Green Fabric - for embroidery and accent strips
- 1/3 yd. Green Hoffman Batik Fabric: FIRST, cut 1 - 6-1/2" square; then cut the remainder into 1" strips

- 7/32" Clothesline Cord: 16 feet for Base and 38 feet for Basket
- 1/2 yd. Light Green Fabric for embroidery and 1" strips
- 1/3 yd. Green Hoffman Batik Fabric: FIRST, cut 1 - 5" x 12" rectangle for the back; then cut remainder into 1" strips for wrapping the cord.

▲ **Bread Basket with a 4" x 11" Center**

▼ Photo Frame with a 5" x 7" Center

Uses the same total yardage as a Trivet, plus:
- Photo Transfer Fabric • One extra piece of Sulky Fuse 'n Stitch
- Coordinating Sulky Blendables® Threads

▼ Bowl

- 7/32" Clothesline Cord - 50 feet
- 1 yd. Light Green Fabric - for embroidery and accent strips
- 1/3 yd. Green Hoffman Batik Fabric: FIRST, cut 1 - 6-1/2" square; then cut the remainder into 1" strips

Bonus! Instructions for these projects are on the CD in the back of this book.

▲ Coasters and Coaster Bowl - Set of 4

- 7/32" Clothesline Cord - 35 feet
- 1/2 yd. Light Green Fabric
- 1/3 yd. Green Batik Fabric

▲ Oval Placemats - Set of 4

- 7/32" Clothesline Cord - approx. 200 feet
- 1- 1/2 yds. Light Batik Fabric
- 1/3 yd. Dark Batik Fabric

1. **Make the thick liquid Solvy solution (see page 71).**

   Paint the light green fabric with the thick liquid Solvy solution.

   Set aside to dry.

2. **Layer the fabric in the appropriate size hoop:**

   A. Bottom hoop on table.
   B. 2 layers of Ultra Solvy lightly misted to hold them together.
   C. Lightly mist the top layer of Ultra Solvy and smooth the prepared light green fabric over it.
   D. Insert top hoop to secure.

3. **Embroider your chosen design**
   using the appropriate Sulky 40 wt. Rayon Thread colors.

**Painting the
Solvy Solution onto Fabric**

- *Dampen the foam brush with water before dipping it in the Solvy solution. (You could substitute a small foam roller.)*
- *Saturate the fabric while brushing in the Solvy solution.*
- *Squeeze any excess Solvy solution from the foam brush onto the fabric and work/brush it in.*
- *If there are any lumps of Solvy solution, remove them with a food scraper, if desired.*
- *Lay the fabric flat to dry.*
- *If you don't have the space to dry the fabric flat, hang the fabric to dry from skirt hangers. While this method can cause the fabric grain to be off, if this happens, iron (steam setting) the fabric until the grain is straight again and let dry. After drying, the fabric will still be stiff but the grain will be back in line.*

4. **Remove the Heavy Stabilizer.**
   Carefully remove (and save) the excess Ultra Solvy, one layer at a time from the back of the embroidery by running a bead of water on a Q-tip along the outer edge of the embroidery design. To remove the painted-on Solvy, fill a top-loading washing machine 1/2 to 3/4 full with warm water, depending on the amount of fabrics.

Agitate on delicate cycle for 1 minute, then soak for 1 hour. Repeat this agitation 3 more times. Leave to soak overnight. In the morning, agitate on delicate cycle again, then spin out. Place the fabrics in a dryer and dry them until they are slightly damp. Press/block until dry.

Create a 5-1/2" Center Base for the Trivet:

Set up the Machine:
- Attach a Closed-toe Appliqué Foot
- Insert a 14/90 Topstitch Needle
- Thread the machine (both top and bobbin) with Sulky White Bobbin Thread
- Select a zig-zag stitch
- Adjust the width - medium to small
- Select a medium length

1. Cut 14 feet of clothesline and fold it in half. Starting at the cut ends, hold both pieces side-by-side,

close together, and zig-zag them together.

2. Cut this joined piece in half when you near the fold in your clothesline.

3. Fold in half again and, starting at the cut ends, zig-zag these sections together. Cut in half when you approach the fold.

> **TIP: Measuring**
> *Nancy is using a 7/32" Wellington cord which measures approximately 3/4" wide when she stitches 4 cords together. Measure the width of your 4 cords as they may compress or widen when stitched together. Adjust the following directions to accommodate the cord you are using.*

4. Cut seven 5-3/4" long pieces from the 4-across, zig-zagged strip. Zig-zag all 7 together to construct the base.

5. Use a 60 mm rotary cutter and quilter's ruler to trim the base to 5-1/2" square.

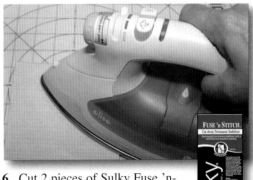

6. Cut 2 pieces of Sulky Fuse 'n-Stitch, each one just slightly shy of 5-1/2" square (so it sits inside your base). Use a medium cotton setting and a dry iron to fuse one piece of Fuse 'n Stitch (the shiny side is the fusible side) onto each side of the 5-1/2" square cord base. Press and hold the iron down until each piece is completely fused.

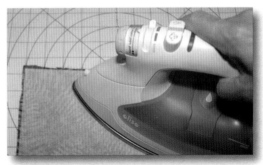

7. Cut two 6-1/2" square pieces of Steam-a-Seam2™. Fuse one to the wrong side of your 6-1/2" square backing fabric. Center the other one on the wrong side of your embroidered fabric and fuse in place.

Place the 5-1/2" square base in the center of the Steam-a-Seam2 on the backing fabric and fuse them together with steam. Fuse the fabric to the base sides, two opposite sides at a time.

76

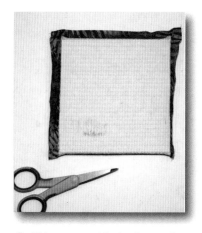

8. Trim even with the front edge of the base, and repeat with the two opposite sides.

Clip corners when all sides are fused and trimmed.

9. Fuse two sides at a time, trim even with the back edge, then fuse the opposite two sides.

Trim and clip all corners.

10. Fuse the Jumbo Fern embroidery in the same manner to the front of the base. To give the embroidery an enhanced 3-dimensional appearance, use a mini-iron to press down the background fabric around the embroidery leaves.

Wrapping the Clothesline:

1. You will need at least 21 feet of clothesline to coil around your center base. Cut the coordinating fabric into 1" strips *(no need to cut on the bias).* Cut off the selvage.

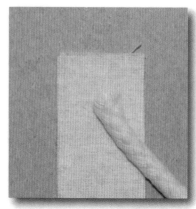

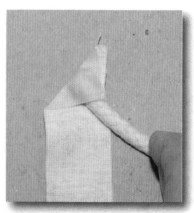

2. Spray Sulky KK 2000 Temporary Spray Adhesive on the wrong side of the first fabric strip end.

3. Place the end of your clothesline at a 45° angle to the fabric strip, pointing at a corner end of it.

4. Fold the fabric corner over the end of the clothesline.

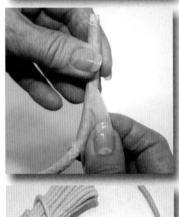

5. Fold the remaining corner over the clothesline and begin wrapping the fabric around the clothesline on a diagonal.

6. The fabric will now be wrapping on the bias. Wrap about a foot at a time and secure the end with a wooden, spring-type clothespin as you continue to stitch.

   To change colors or add a second strip of fabric, with the wrong side of the fabric facing you, trim the right hand corner to reduce bulk.

   Spray KK 2000 on about 1" of the end of the wrong side of the new strip, and begin wrapping it over the first fabric strip on the clothesline in the same spiral-wrapped direction, making sure that none of the clothesline is showing through.

1. Start at the right top or bottom corner, leaving the end extending just slightly past the corner because it tends to pull back just a bit, and the very end is mostly fabric that will compress.

2. To hold the wrapped clothesline snug against the side of the base, stick a straight pin into it.

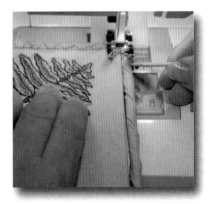

Adding Wrapped Clothesline to the Trivet Base:

Set up the Machine:
- Attach a Closed-toe Appliqué Foot
- Insert a 16/100 Denim Needle
- Wind a Bobbin and Thread the Top with Sulky 30 wt. Cotton Blendables #4019

Forest Floor
- Select a multi-stitch zig-zag
- Medium width and length

Nancy likes to use 7 to 8 wrapped fabric rows stitched onto a 5-1/2" center base to make a nice-sized trivet. (See page 73)

3. Use the Jeans-A-Ma-Jig accessory to level the back side of the presser foot, if necessary. Begin stitching, using a stiletto or bamboo skewer to hold the cord flat to the base as you begin to stitch.

4. When you arrive at the next corner, stop with the needle down in the cord in the center of the presser foot. Turn and replace the Jeans-a-Ma-Jig (if necessary) under the back and side to level the presser foot.

Begin stitching and repeat this as you go around all 4 sides.

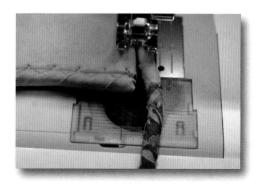

> **TIP:** *If you decide you want to change fabric, wait until you approach the corner where you started, then change your fabric so that your next color starts just after the first wrap. Then, as you turn the corner once again, you will have one complete row of one color.*

5. To keep your project square and balanced, always change the fabric color at the corner where you began, and finish your tapered end at that same corner after you finish your last row.

6. When finishing, cut your clothesline at a long angle at the beginning corner. Spread glue stick on about the last 2 inches of the fabric.

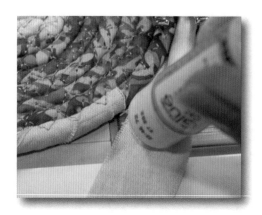

7. Wrap the fabric strip around and past the end of the clothesline, angling it into a fabric taper. Zig-zag off the tapered end.

Have fun trying all types of fabric combinations.
Add little fabric cut-outs like these dragonflies.

Holiday Corded Crafts

You can also make Holiday Corded Crafts like these. Just substitute a theme fabric for the embroidered Fern. They make quick, hostess gifts!

Jumbo Fern Bread Basket

Materials:

Same as Jumbo Fern Trivet, except you need approximately 55 feet of Wellington clothesline and approximately 1/2 yard of various fabrics.

Use the Trivet Directions on page 76 to construct the bread basket base but change the dimension of the center base to 4" x 11".

Make the Corded Bread Basket:

1. Fold 19 feet of cord in half and zig-zag together. Fold in half again and zig-zag again, making a 4-cord-across strip.

2. Cut five 11-1/4" pieces from the 4-cord strip. Zig-zag all 5 cut pieces together to construct the base.

3. The balance of the base construction directions are the same as the trivet directions.

Boston Compacta

1. Using a fern print fabric, attach the cord to the base in the same manner as in the trivet directions; zig-zag two rows on.

2. Change to an open-toe appliqué foot.

3. After these two rows are completed and you are at the corner where you began, cut strips from the same fabric on which you embroidered the Jumbo Ferns. Tilt the base upward with your left hand, and hold the base against the side of your sewing machine while you continue to wrap these fabric strips around the cord and zig-zag your rows together. Add seven more rows.

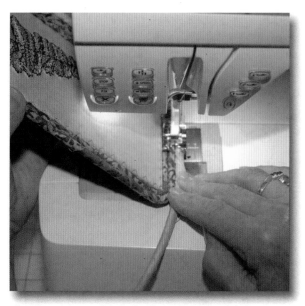

4. Change your fabric back to the same fabric you used for your first two rows. Add two more rows and finish with a taper at the starting corner (total 11 rows).

TIP: *An open-toe appliqué foot will give you more flexibility for a variety of angles. By lifting your working (loose, wrapped) cord slightly, you can achieve a flatter side to your bowl or basket.*

Orphan Block Trivets

Don't throw away that leftover quilt block or practice embroidery! They make perfect centers for Corded Trivets. Cheater prints work well too. Be creative with your leftovers!

Paper-Fabric Collage

Have you ever admired those hand-made Journals, Notepads and Boxes in fancy boutiques? Well, now you can make your own following any theme you desire. It's easy using Carol's instructions.

Carol Ingram, on the right, with Pokey Bolton taping a PBS "*Quilting Arts*" TV program.

Materials:

- Sulky Cut-Away Plus Stabilizer
- 8" Roll of Sulky Solvy or Super Solvy Stabilizer
- Sulky Threads
- Inexpensive Paint Brush
- Inks and Sponge-Tip Applicators
- Oil Paint Sticks – Stencil Brush
- Paper selection – colored tissue paper, scrapbook papers, newspaper, magazine photos, copy paper photos, old wrapping paper, old tissue dress patterns
- A non-stick surface, i.e. plastic tablecloth, Teflon pressing sheet or wax paper
- Velcro Dots
- Two-sided Sticky Tape
- Blank notepads, journals or sticky notes
- Eyelets and eyelet tool
- Ribbons, cords, and beads for couching and embellishing
- General Supplies

by Carol Ingram

Featuring Sulky® *Liquid* Solvy™
and Cut-Away Plus™ Stabilizers.

Make Carol's "Solvy Glop" Paste

"Use one whole 8" roll of Solvy. Unroll and fold it over itself many times, then use a rotary cutter to cut crosswise over it both ways to make tiny pieces like confetti.

Put the Solvy confetti in a plastic container. Add enough very hot water to mix the confetti (stir with a spoon or brush) into a thick, runny paste. Stir until all small pieces are smooth for spreading. Do not whip or use an electric mixer because it will become foamy and/or change the consistency of the paste. We want runny paste not foamy liquid." - Carol

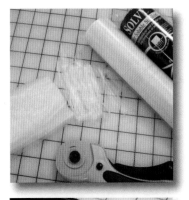

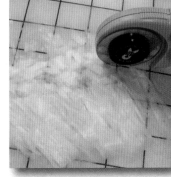

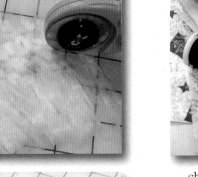

choose a color that will enhance the project colors since the tissue paper becomes transparent and makes a new color, unless you use white.

Cover the tabletop with a non-stick surface.

1. First layer - Cut a piece of dyed Cut-Away Plus to the desired size. Use an inexpensive paint brush to spread a layer of Sulky liquid Solvy "Glop" over the Cut-Away Plus; saturate the entire piece.

2. While it is wet, lay one or two layers of your choice of paper on top of it. Choose the paper (tissue paper, newspaper, wrapping paper, etc.) that works best for your project. If you use tissue paper,

3. Use a brush to saturate the added paper with another layer of Solvy "Glop".

4. Let dry overnight or outside in the sunshine.

86

5. Once dried, if the paper has curled, iron the piece and place it under a stack of books to undo any curls on the edges.

6. Turn the project over and lay it back on a protected surface.

7. Spread a layer of Solvy "Glop" with a brush.

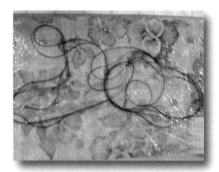

8. Toss loose Sulky decorative threads into the wet Solvy "Glop".

9. Add a layer of tissue paper over the threads. *Choose a tissue paper color that will enhance the project colors since the tissue paper becomes transparent and makes a new color, unless you use white tissue.*

10. Spread another layer of Solvy "Glop" and add more loose Sulky threads or other found items to have your desired textural effect on the 2nd side.

11. Again, let dry overnight or outside in the sunshine. Another drying method (recommended only for the second side) is to heat your oven to high, then **turn it off;** place the project on a cookie sheet and put it in the warm oven until it is dry.

12. Decide which side will be the inside, and place the item you are covering (i.e. journal, book, calendar, notepad covers, bookmarks etc.) on the dried, prepared base; use a chalk marker to draw around the edges to indicate the boundaries of the item you have chosen. Fold over your book, etc., to be sure that you have the margin you want extending around it. If not, add 1/4" or so all around to your traced outline, and test again.

13. Further embellish the outside to your taste within the drawn boundaries, using decorative stitches, random free-motion stitching, couching ribbons or cords, adding sequins, beads or other found items.

14. Cut out the pattern, straight stitch around the outside edge, if desired, and fold into the bookcover, notepad or binder. Add Velcro fasteners, eyelet fasteners or ribbon ties.

15. If your project is a notepad or binder, attach the notepads or tablets inside with two-sided sticky tape.

Introduction to Recipes for Quilters

by Bev Morris and Nancy Bryant
Owners of Abigayle's Stitchery in Olmsted Falls, OH, and primary contributors to
"Weekend Quilting with Sulky", Book #900B-16

"Abigayle's Quiltery is a premier quilt shop in Northern Ohio. We started this shop in 1999 with the desire for the very best in quilting, sewing and embroidery. We have always thrived in a creative environment and wanted to share our passion for sewing with everyone. We like to believe that like-minded creative people are drawn to Abigayle's and so it was... the ladies from Sulky came to our store when they first came to Cleveland to tape a PBS-TV show! We have had many years of sewing weekends with them since that first encounter and we are blessed with great, creative and motivating friends in Sulky.

Since we are self-confessed 'quilt snobs', we will only accept the best in products for our store and customers. We chose Sulky to be one of those very few lines that we carry in its entirety. The always reliable results of Sulky products serve the diverse needs of our customers well. Choosy customers find that Sulky's range of products, high quality, reasonable prices and educational information meet their extensive range of needs.

Blanket Stitch Appliqué -
Sulky Tear-Easy is our favorite to ensure consistent success with blanket stitch appliqué and decorative stitching – favorites at Abigayle's. Spray Sulky KK 2000 on the Tear-Easy, place it behind the background fabric, and viola! – no pins necessary and flat appliqué blocks. This easily-removed product stabilizes the stitching but does not create bulk in the end project.

T-Shirt Quilts -
T-Shirt quilts present a unique problem in that they utilize a knit fabric that is quite stretchy – very different from the cottons that quilters usually use. These knits must be stabilized to promote the longevity of the quilt and to stabilize the seam for flawless stitching. Sulky Tender Touch is just light enough to provide stability while maintaining the softness of the original fabrics.

Turned Edge Appliqué -
We also love Sulky Tender Touch to prepare appliqués for stitching. Whether you use your blind hem stitch and Sulky Polyester Invisible Thread, or embellish your appliqué with a decorative stitch, the edges are turned under flawlessly and secured for a perfect appliqué finish. Needle-turn appliquérs love this technique because they can just concern themselves with getting a perfect stitch and not turning the fabric under. Try this technique with a hand blanket stitch and Sulky 12 wt. Cotton Thread for a very traditional result.

Redwork -
We use Tender Touch to line any "show-through" fabrics. White on white fabrics are prone to seam allowance shadowing. Redwork with Sulky 30 wt. Cotton Thread looks crisp and pristine on a white background supported with Sulky Tender Touch. Also, because it is an iron-on product, it secures the loose threads and prevents fraying.

Purses and Totes -
Quilters of all ages love to make fast and fashionable purses. To create and maintain that designer look, the purse bottoms and handles need to be properly stabilized. We highly recommend Sulky Fuse 'n Stitch for handles and just about any reinforcement on the purse. You'll love the professional results!

Paper Piecing -
Did you know that you can print directly onto Sulky Paper Solvy? Two of the most time-consuming aspects of paper piecing are transferring the design to a sewable paper and then later, the tedium of tearing it away. Often the tearing away process distorts and damages the stitches. Paper Solvy washes away without distressing the sewn work.

Quilting -
Many quilters love to use Sulky Solvy to mark the quilting designs for their quilt. Simply transfer the design to Solvy, stitch, and wash away. You'll be so happy when you don't have to deal with those annoying pencil marks! When we put the quilt layers together, instead of pinning or basting, we love, love, love Sulky KK 2000. It is environmentally friendly, non-toxic, odorless and a real timesaver. Students have superior quilting results because KK 2000 prevents slipping and puckering."

88

"Ribbons of Thread"

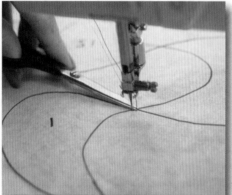

Recipe for Success

Quilter:
Libby Lehman
*Award winning Quilter,
Teacher, Artist*

Needle:
• Schmetz Topstitch, Size 14/90

Thread:
• Beautiful Sulky 40 wt. Rayon and Metallics

Stabilizer:
• Sulky Totally Stable™ - iron-on, temporary

Procedure:
In the book, "Quilting Concepts in Sulky", Libby used Sulky Rayon and Metallic Threads along with Sulky Totally Stable as a quilting embellishment guide.
• Use a permanent-ink marker to trace your design onto the non-fusible side of Sulky Totally Stable.
• Fuse the stabilizer onto the pieced quilt top.
• Thread the machine with Sulky Rayon or Metallic Thread and put Sulky Polyester Invisible Thread in the bobbin.
• Set up for Free-Motion.
• Use a short stitch length and stitch along the design lines.
• Remove the excess stabilizer.

The complete book and patterns are available on DVD -
"Quilting Concepts in Sulky"
visit: www.sulky.com

"Mother Earth Meets
Ocean Depth"

Recipe for Success

**Quilter:
Heidi Lund**
Fiber Artist

Needle:
- Schmetz Topstitch, Size 14/90

Thread:
- Beautiful Sulky 40 wt. Rayon and Metallics

Stabilizer:
- Sulky Totally Stable™ - iron-on, temporary

Procedure:
Heidi uses Sulky Totally Stable as a backing when free-motion quilting.

- Simply iron a piece of Totally Stable to the back of the fleece.
- The Totally Stable will keep the piece stable while providing a slick surface to ride over the throat plate of the machine. No stress, no snags, no pulling, no problems!

Visit: www.heidilund.com
*Look for Heidi's Blendables®
Designer Thread Collection
"Life in the Tropics".*

"The Red Jacket"

*Winner of Judge's Choice &
Viewer's Choice Awards at the
International Quilt Festival
in Houston, TX*

Faux Fur

Recipe for Success

**Quilter:
Janelle Archer**
*Award-winning Quilter
and Fiber Artist*

Needle:
• Schmetz Topstitch, Size 14/90

Thread:
• Beautiful Sulky 40 wt. Rayon
  and Sulky Holoshimmer™
  Metallic Threads

Stabilizer:
• Sulky Solvy™ - water soluble
• Sulky KK 2000™ Temporary Spray Adhesive

Procedure:
*Janelle uses Sulky Solvy as a topper when making
faux fur for insets, collars, cuffs, muffs, etc.*

• Use a base of silk organza that is sprayed with
  Sulky KK 2000 and layer pieces of yarns in the
  same color palette as the project on which it will
  be placed.
• After laying about 4 layers of yarn and/or when
  the base is completely covered, spray it again with
  KK 2000.
• Smooth a layer of Solvy over all of it.
• Straight stitch a grid over it. Then, random stitch
  all over it several times with different Sulky
  Rayon and Metallic Threads, making sure to catch
  all the yarn.
• Remove the Solvy by submerging in warm water.
• When completely dry, cut to size to fit the project.

91

"Lara's Coat - Dr. Zhivago
in the 21st. Century"

Fairfield Fashion Show
Houston, TX

92

"Allegretto"

"My latest quilt is a combination of a painted canvas and a quilt made to look like a painting." --- Katie

Holding Pieces

Recipe for Success

Quilter:
Katie Pasquini Masopust
Speaker, Teacher, Artist and Author

Needle:
• Schmetz Topstitch, Size 14/90

Thread:
• Sulky Polyester Clear Invisible

Stabilizer:
• Sulky Totally Stable™
  - iron-on, temporary

Procedure:
Katie loves using Sulky Totally Stable to hold down her pieces until she stitches them.

• Draw your design on the fusible side of Totally Stable.
• Put the turned edge pieces of your appliqués in their positions and touch the tip of the iron to them to hold them in place.
• When about a square foot is complete, turn it over and press from the back to hold everything securely in place. Repeat until finished.
• Set the machine for free-motion.
• Use a free-motion, zig-zag stitch to stitch everything down with Sulky Clear Polyester Invisible Thread.

Visit Katie: www.katiepm.com

Recipe for Success

Quilter:
M'Liss Rae Hawley
Fabric Expert and Author

Needle:
- Topstitching, Size 14/90

Thread:
- Sulky 40 wt. Rayon

Stabilizer:
- Sulky Stiffy™ - tear-away

Procedure: *"Embroidered Windows"*

Since stabilizing is the key to perfect embroidery, M'Liss prefers to use 2 layers of Sulky Stiffy, a crisp, tear-away stabilizer, when embroidering blocks for quilts.

Working with batiks, she used analogous colors (colors next to each other on the color wheel) and, to make them stand out even more, added red to frame the embroideries. Before she attached the border to the quilt, she embroidered her "Morning Glory Trellis" motif on two border strips of fabric, then placed them asymmetrically on the quilt for a more artistic look.

When you complete your embroideries, M'Liss suggests you press them with the right side down on a terry towel.

She offset the quilt blocks to give the illusion that the embroideries are floating. By stipple quilting the background around the embroidery, it makes the embroidered motif seem to "pop"… a nice visual.

94

"Sea Life"

"This was one of those "UFP's"
unfinished projects. It finally found
its time to shine when I quilted it with
Sulky Holoshimmer and
Sulky 30 wt. Cotton". --- Eric

Transfer Quilt Designs

Recipe for Success

Quilter: Eric Drexler
National Sulky Educator

Needle:
• Schmetz Topstitch, Size 14/90

Threads:
• Sulky 30 wt. Cotton
• Sulky Holoshimmer™ Metallic

Stabilizer:
• Sulky Super Solvy™ - water soluble
• Sulky KK 2000™ Temporary Spray Adhesive

Procedure:
Eric likes to use unique quilt designs.
Here is how he got the wave that he
used throughout the quilt pictured on
this page and on the previous page.

• The quilt was pieced using Sulky 30 wt. Cotton.
• Using an ultra-fine-line, permanent-ink marker, the waves were traced from a ceramic tile design onto strips of Sulky Super Solvy cut from an 8" roll. (Since Super Solvy can be pressed with a hot iron, you could use a Sulky Iron-On Transfer Pen instead to make multiple Solvy patterns.)
• The back of the Super Solvy strips were sprayed with Sulky KK 2000, then finger-pressed in position on the quilt. (KK 2000 makes it easy to reposition the Solvy quilt template, if necessary.) The strips were placed one at a time, and the wave was free-motion stitched onto the quilt with a Sulky 30 wt. solid-color Cotton Thread.
• The Super Solvy was easily torn away.

If you stand very still in the heart
of the woods, you will hear many
wonderful things . . . the snap of a twig
and the wind in the trees, and the whir
of invisible wings.

If you stand very still in the turmoil
of life, and you wait for a voice from
within, you'll be led down the quiet ways,
of wisdom and peace in a mad world
of chaos and din.

If you stand very still and hold to
your faith, you will get all the help
that you ask; you will draw from the
silence the things that you need.

Hope, Courage and Strength
for your task.   *Candance Kelly*

"Stand in the Woods"

*"I love to use Paper Solvy for all my paper piecing
projects. You can copy the pattern onto it by running
it through a copy machine instead of regular paper.
It stabilizes the pieces through the ironing process
and assembly and then washes away, saving you
time and trouble." --- Joyce*

Paper Piecing

Recipe for Success

Quilter: Joyce Drexler
Artist, Author, TV Personality

Needle:
• Schmetz Topstitch, Size 12/80

Thread:
• Sulky PolyLite™ 60 wt. Thread

Stabilizer:
• Sulky Paper-Solvy - water soluble

Procedure:
• Place the original design in a copy machine.
• In place of copy paper, substitute as many sheets
  of Sulky Paper Solvy as you need for your project.
• After you make your copies on the Paper Solvy, do
  your paper piecing on them using ultra-fine Sulky
  PolyLite 60 wt. Thread. The Paper Solvy stabilizes the pieces through the ironing and assembly
  processes, and the PolyLite allows for a perfect
  crease without adding any bulk.
• When the piecing is completed, simply submerge
  in warm water and the Paper Solvy will dissolve
  away, saving you time and eliminating any
  possible pull-out of thread that
  can occur when tearing away
  normal paper patterns.
• Lay flat to dry.
• Piece into your project.

Complete directions to make
this project can be found in the
book: *"An Updated Supplement to Sulky's Secrets to
Successful Stabilizing"* -
#900B-17

97

Quilter:
Valerie
Hearder

International Art Quilter
and Author

Recipe for Success

"The key advantage to using Fabri-Solvy is that it holds the confetti in place and is firm enough to machine stitch without using a hoop - then it washes away."

Needle:
- Schmetz Topstitch, Size 12/80

Thread:
- Sulky Polyester Clear Invisible
- Sulky 30 wt. Rayon

Stabilizer:
- Sulky Fabri-Solvy™ - water soluble

Procedure:
- To make the leaves on the tree, slice up green fabric into tiny fragments with a rotary cutter.
- Sprinkle the confetti onto a base of organza.
- Draw an outline of the crown of the tree onto one layer of Sulky Fabri-Solvy.
- Sandwich the fabric and organza between 2 layers of Fabri-Solvy with the crown drawing on top.
- Free-motion stitch in circles catching all the confetti.
- Rinse away the Fabri-Solvy.

98

T-Shirt Quilt

Recipe for Success

Quilter:
Sue Selby Moats

*Long-arm Quilter,
Freelance National
Educator*

Representing Sulky of America

Needle:
- Schmetz Embroidery, Size 12/80

Threads:
- Sulky Poly Deco™ or Sulky PolyLite™

Stabilizer:
- Sulky Tender Touch™ - iron-on, permanent

Procedure:
- Sulky Tender Touch was fused onto the wrong side of each T-shirt before it was cut and sewn into the quilt.
- This gives the T-shirt a much nicer body to work with while sewing and/or quilting, but leaves the shirt very soft and pliable.

"You Can Walk However You Like!"

Breast Cancer Awareness Quilt

The quilt on the next page was constructed of T-shirts donated by Cancer Survivors from ACS Making Strides Against Breast Cancer; ACS Relay for Life; Avon Walk for Hope and the Komen Race for the Cure.

Quilt for a Cure Healing Garden Fabrics (representing plants used in cancer treatment) are used in the sashing and borders of the quilt. These were designed by Bonnie Benn Stratton in the late 1990's in honor of her friend Lenore Parham, who died of cancer. Lenore and her husband Walter talked of a garden with plants used for healing cancer. Walter had the garden developed in a park in Northern Virginia in her memory.

Many words are included in the quilting:
- *Relay for Life*
- *Honor*
- *Celebrate Life*
- *Remember*
- *Laugh*
- *Love*
- *Hope*
- *Walk for Hope*

While October is Breast Cancer Awareness Month, other events to raise funds for Cancer research, diagnosis and treatment are held throughout the year. Please support the Cancer Walk or other events for the cause of your choice to help find a cure for this disease.

99

Celebrate Life -
Breast Cancer Awareness T-Shirt Quilt made by Sue Moats

Recipe for Success

Quilter:
Judy Lowery

Franklin, NC

Stabilizer:

- Sulky Tender Touch™ - iron-on, permanent

Procedure:

- Sulky Tender Touch was fused onto each T-shirt before it was cut and sewn into the quilt.
- This gives the T-shirt a much nicer body to work with while sewing and/or quilting, but leaves the shirt very soft and pliable.

"Rockin' in the 70's" was made for Judy's Grandson, Alex Pritscher from a collection of his favorite musician T-shirts.

"Miles and Miles of Memories" was made for Jim Sheppard of Toledo, OH a *Harley Davidson™* enthusiastic.

"Cheerleader's School Spirit" was made for Ginger Parks who is the coach for the cheerleaders at Newsome High School in Plant City, FL.

"Rockin' in the 70's"

"Miles and Miles of Memories"

by Nancy Sapin & Joyce Drexler

Featuring: Joyce Drexler's "Preferred Greens" Designer Rayon Thread Collection,
Sulky Tender Touch™, and Sulky Heat-Away Clear Film™.   Finished size: Approximately 14-1/2" square.

Flower Power

Want to make some quick and easy pillows for yourself or for gifts? This one you can make in one afternoon!

Materials:

- 1/4 yard of light green fabric
- 3/4 yard of green fern print
- Sulky Heat-Away Clear Film
  (1) 6" square and (4) 2" x 10" strips
- Sulky Tender Touch (1) 16" square,
  (2) 11" x 15-1/2" pieces,
  and enough 1-1/2" wide strips to
  equal at least 65" (for piping)
- Sulky KK 2000™ Temporary Spray
  Adhesive
- Sulky Holoshimmer™ Metallic
  #6032 Lime Green
- Sulky 40 wt. Rayon Threads from
  Joyce Drexler's "Preferred Greens"
  Designer Thread Collection
- Sulky White Bobbin Thread or one
  of the green Rayon Threads
- 16" Square of Batting
- 14/90 Metallic or Topstitch Needle
- Free-motion, Spring-loaded Presser
  Foot
- Zipper Foot
- Ditch Stitching Presser Foot or
  Walking Foot
- 1/4" Presser Foot for Piecing
- At least 65" of 1/4" Cord for Piping
- General Sewing Supplies
- 14" Pillow Form (optional)

You will learn the following techniques:

- Use Sulky Heat-Away as a pattern for free-motion
  stitching.
- Stitch-in-the-ditch using Sulky Holoshimmer™
  Metallic Decorative Thread.
- Free-motion outline stitching using two Sulky Rayon
  threads in one needle at the same time.
- Make your own matching decorative pillow piping.
- Learn how to add extra body to your fabric pillow
  back and piping fabric by adding Sulky Tender Touch.

Cutting Directions:

Light Green Fabric:
- (1) 4-1/2" square for center block
- (2) 1-1/2" x 6-1/2" pieces
- (2) 1-1/2" x 8-1/2" pieces
- (2) 1-3/4" x width-of-fabric strips for piping

Green Fern Print Fabric:
- (2) 1-1/2" x 4-1/2" pieces
- (2) 1-1/2" x 6-1/2" pieces
- (2) 4" x 8-1/2" pieces
- (2) 4" x 15-1/2" pieces
- (2) 11" x 15-1/2" pieces for back

Piecing the Pillow Top Together:

1. Attach a 1/4" presser foot and set the machine for a straight stitch with a 2.2 stitch length. With right sides together, stitch one 1-1/2" x 4-1/2" green fern fabric to each of the two opposite sides of a 4-1/2" square, light green center block; press seams to the dark fabric.

2. With right sides together, stitch one 1-1/2" x 6-1/2" green fern fabric to each of the top and bottom of your light green center block; press seams to the dark fabric.

3. With right sides together, stitch one 1-1/2" x 6-1/2" light green fabric to each of the two opposite sides of your 6-1/2" square center block; press seams to the dark fabric.

4. With right sides together, stitch one 1-1/2" x 8-1/2" light green fabric to the top and bottom of your center block; press seams to the dark fabric. Stitch one 4" x 8-1/2" green fern fabric to each of

the two opposite sides of your 8-1/2" square center block; press seams to the dark fabric.

5. With right sides together, stitch one 4" x 15-1/2" green fern fabric to each of the top and bottom of your center block; press seams to the dark fabric.

Making your Quilt Sandwich:

1. Place the bumpy side of a 16" square of Tender Touch against a 16" square of batting and fuse them together. With the right side up, lay the pieced pillow top on the opposite side of the batting that has the Tender Touch fused to it.

2. Fold half of the pillow top back on itself and lightly spray Sulky KK 2000 onto the wrong side of the pillow top; unfold and smooth in place.

Repeat with the other half to complete the quilt sandwich. The smoothness of Sulky Tender Touch will also aid in free-motion movement, in addition to helping to support a multitude of stitches.

Spring has sprung with this explosion of flowers on fabric. Choose a fabric that best suits your decor.

105

Stitch-In-The-Ditch:

1. Attach either a ditch-stitching foot or a walking foot and set your machine for a straight stitch with a 3.0 stitch length.

2. Place Sulky Holoshimmer on your machine's vertical spool pin so the thread stays flat as it feeds into your machine. Wind the bobbin with Sulky White Bobbin Thread or one of your Green Rayons.

3. For a more decorative appearance, stitch in the ditch of all of the seams. Always practice first since you may have to reduce your upper thread tension along with making sure the flat thread is correctly feeding into your machine.

Heat-Away Clear Film Free-motion Tracing:

1. Use an ultra-fine, permanent-ink marker to trace Joyce Drexler's Abstract Flower pattern (found on the CD at the back of this book) onto the smooth side of a 6" square of Sulky Heat-Away Clear Film.

2. Lightly spray KK 2000 onto the 4" light green square of the pillow top. With the bumpy side of the Heat-Away against the fabric, center the traced design over the 4" square. Attach a spring-loaded, free-motion foot or darning foot. Thread the top with Sulky 40 wt. Rayon #1176, and the bobbin with Sulky White Bobbin Thread or a green Rayon.

3. Use a free-motion straight stitch to stitch over the design in one continuous motion; start in the center, double back over the tendrils, trace around each petal of the flower a second time, and end back in the center where you began. Lock your beginning and ending stitches. Remove from the machine.

4. Gently tear away any excess borders of the Heat-Away. With your iron set on a medium cotton setting, use the tip of the iron to heat away the stabilizer with a continuous circular movement until all of the Heat-Away has melted into tiny balls, which you can easily brush away or remove with a lint roller. (Always test first on a scrap quilt sandwich so you know the proper setting for your iron). Thread the top with Holoshimmer #6032 Lime and free-motion straight stitch the design one or two more times around to your liking.

5. From the pattern on the CD at the back of this book, trace the inner border diagonal lines onto all four 2" x 10" strips of Heat-Away. Use KK 2000 to secure each strip, one at a time, to the light green border strips of the pillow top. Attach a straight stitch or walking foot and raise the feed dogs. Use Holoshimmer #6032 Lime to stitch over the lines from one edge of the light green strip to the other, making sure the corner lines reach from each outer corner to inner corner. Gently tear away what you can, then apply the next strip; repeat until all 4 border strips are finished. Heat away any remaining stabilizer. KK 2000 also dissipates with dry heat ... *such a great match!*

Make the Matching Piping:

1. Use the same presser foot and thread the top with all-purpose sewing thread. Place the long ends of two 1-3/4" x width-of-fabric strips of light green fabric, right sides together, and stitch them together; cut to make one 65" long strip.

Tender Touch on the wrong side of strip

2. Cut several 1-1/2" strips of Sulky Tender Touch and butt them together, end to end (fusible side down), on the wrong side of the 65" piping strip; fuse them together. Thread the top with Holoshimmer #6032 Lime and straight stitch a large zig-zag pattern on the right side of your piping strip. When you reach the end, create diamond shapes by straight stitching the same zig-zag pattern opposite what you just did. Set aside.

Outlining the Fern Fabric Print:

1. Attach a spring-loaded, free-motion foot or darning foot. Thread two Sulky Rayon threads #630 Moss Green and #1276 Pistachio through the top and into a single needle. With a free-motion straight stitch, practice outlining the design pattern of some of your extra fabric print. When you are satisfied with your technique, do the same on the actual project, including the inner border. You don't need to outline each one, just here and there, all in a continuous movement.

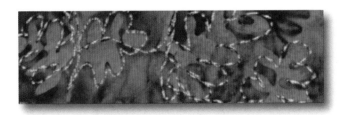

2. Change the top threads to #1176 Med. Dk. Avocado and #1209 Lt. Avocado and stitch some more, which gives a nice contrast and a twisted thread appearance. Free-motion outline the pattern of your fabric ferns in places that you did not do previously, which gives a slightly illusionary, dimensional appearance. Again, no need to do them all, just here and there. When you are satisfied, trim the pillow top to 15" square.

Create the Pillow Back:

1. Fuse an 11" x 15" piece of Tender Touch onto the wrong side of each of the two 11" x 15" pieces of green fern fabric. On the shorter 11" side of one fused piece, fold a 3/4" fold to the wrong side and press. Fold over another 3/4" fold to make this piece 9-1/2" x 15"; press. Do this for both pieces to provide plenty of overlap when you insert your pillow form.

2. Let's make it decorative . . . With the same two Rayon Threads in the needle, choose one of your decorative stitches and stitch along your folded fabric, or use a straight stitch, if you prefer.

Finish the Piping:

1. Change to an all-purpose sewing thread and attach the zipper foot (left bar) without changing the needle position. With wrong sides together, fold the length of the piping fabric in half, around a 65" piece of 1/4" cord; straight stitch the fabric together, matching the raw edges as you stitch.

2. Without changing the needle position, match all the raw edges as you begin to stitch the piping onto the right side of the pillow top, just past where you wish to end. Clip the piping fabric seam allowance as you turn each corner. Butt together both the beginning and ending of the piping as tightly as possible and stitch across to where you began.

Attach the Backing:

1. With right sides together, pin one of the 9-1/2" x 15" pillow backs to any one end of the pillow top. Pin the other 9-1/2" x 15" pillow back to the opposite end of the pillow top so the stitched folds of each pillow back overlap in the center to create the opening for turning, and to insert a pillow form.

2. Move your needle position as far left as possible. Use a stiletto or bamboo skewer to apply pressure against the inside of the piping cord to move it as far left (toward the center of the pillow) as possible. Straight stitch as tightly as possible against the piping while moving slowly around the corners.

3. Once completed, change to an appliqué/zig-zag foot and zig-zag close to the edges and tighter to the piping at the corners. Clip the corners next to the zig-zag stitch and turn right side out. Insert a 14" pillow form (optional to add extra stuffing into the corners) and enjoy the beauty of your labor.

Quaking Aspens

This wallhanging incorporates strip-piecing, printable fabric sheets, free-motion thread painting, and free-form thread appliqués. Finished Size: 12-1/2" x 19-1/2"

You can also purchase the Tree and Leaf as a digitized design by joining the **Sulky Embroidery Design Club.**

by *Eric Drexler*

National Sulky Educator and T.V. Personality

Featuring Sulky® Totally Stable, Fabri-Solvy, and Soft 'n Sheer Stabilizers.

Layout:

Use a 1/4" Seam Allowance throughout.

D	L	D	L	D	L	D	L	D	L	D	L	D	L
L					L			A					D
D					D								L
L					L								D
D		E			D	L	D	L	D	L	D	L
L					L								D
D					D			B					L
L					L								D
D					D								L
L					L								D
D	L	D	L	D	L	D	L	D	L	D	L	D	L
L	F Use a photo that				L								D
D	has been printed			D								L
L	onto printable fabric,			L								D
D	L or use a coordinating	L	D	D		C					L
L	print.				L								D
D		G			D								L
L					L								D
D	L	D	L	D	L	D	L	D	L	D	L	D	L

Materials for Quilt Top:

Fabrics:
- 1/2 yd. of a **LIGHT (L)** coordinating print cut into 7 - 1-1/2" x 22" strips and 3 - 2" x 42" strips for binding
- 3/4 yd. of a **DARK (D)** solid fabric:
  Cut 4 - 1-1/2" x 44" strips -
  Then cut them in half to make
  8 - 1-1/2" x 22" strips
  Then cut:
  1 - 5-1/2" x 9-1/4" piece (**E**)
  1 - 6-1/2" x 7-1/4" piece (**C**)
  1 - 14-1/2" x 19-1/2" piece for backing
- 1 - 5-1/2" x 6-1/2" coordinating print (**B**)
- 1/8 yd. light coordinating solid:
  Cut: 1 - 3-1/2" x 5-1/2" piece (**G**)
  Cut: 1 - 3-1/2" x 6-1/2" piece (**A**)
- 1 sheet of Printed Treasures™ Ink-Jet Printable Fabric Sheets.
  After printing: Cut to 3-1/2" x 5-1/2" (**F**)
- 1 - 8-1/2" x 11" piece of Silk Organza
- Batting & Backing - 15" x 20"

Sulky Stabilizer:
- 1 - 8-1/2" x 11" piece of Sulky Totally Stable™ Iron-on Stabilizer

Notions:
- Sulky KK 2000™ Temporary Spray Adhesive
- Sulky 30 wt. Cotton Blendables® Thread Colors:
  #4044 Butterscotch and
  #4011 Milk Chocolate
- Sulky PolyLite 60 wt. Polyester Thread
- Seam Ripper and Quilter's Straight Pins
- Schmetz Denim Needle, Size 14/90
- Rotary Cutter, Ruler and Mat
- Iron and Ironing Surface
- Hand Needle & 4 Safety Pins
- Colored Photo and Typed Words

Machine Feet:
- Free-Motion Quilting Foot
- Quarter Inch Foot
- All Purpose Foot

Piecing Instructions:

1. With right sides together, piece alternating 1-1/2" x 22" **DARK** (D) solid strips with 1-1/2" x 22" **LIGHT** (L) printed strips.

2. Press seams to one side. Cut one end even, then cut across the pieced set into 1-1/2" strip-sets.

3. Unsew small squares from a strip-set as needed to make two 6-square strips that begin with an (L) and end with a (D).

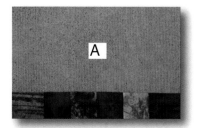

4. With right sides together, sew the 6-1/2" side of (A) to the first 6-square strip-set made in #3. Press the seam to one side.

5. With right sides together, sew the other side of the strip-set to the 6-1/2" side of (B). Press the seam to one side.

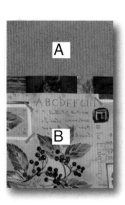

6. With right sides together, sew the other 6-1/2" side of (B) to the second 6-square strip-set made in #3. Press the seam to one side.

7. With right sides together, sew the other side of the 6-square strip-set to the 6-1/2" side of (C). Press the seam to one side.

8. Unsew the small squares from a strip set as needed to make two 5-square strip-sets that begin and end with a light (L) print square.

9. With right sides together, sew the 5-1/2" side of (E) to the first 5-square strip-set made in #8. Press the seam to one side.

10. With right sides together, sew the other side of the strip-set to the 5-1/2" side of (F). Press the seam to one side.

11. With right sides together, sew the other side of (F) to the second 5-square strip-set from #8. Press the seam to one side.

12. With right sides together, sew the other side of the 5-square strip-set to the 5-1/2" side of (G). Press the seam to one side.

13. With right sides together, sew two 1-1/2" pieced strip-sets together, end-to-end, so the **LIGHT** (L) and **DARK** (D) alternate. Unsew as needed to create a 17 square strip-set starting and ending with a light (L) square.

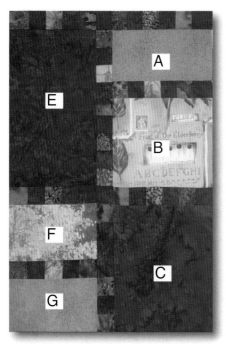

14. With right sides together, sew the 17-square strip-set to the long side of the pieced section from #12, matching seams where the vertical strip-set squares meet the horizontal strip-set squares. Sew. Press seams to one side.

15. With right sides together, sew the long side of the joined section from #14 to the left side of the joined section from #8.

Check to make sure the finished piece is "squared" up. Block if needed to attain the correct shape.

16. With right sides together, sew two 1-1/2" pieced strip-sets together, end-to-end, so they alternate between (L) and (D). Unsew to create a 12-square strip-set that begins with an (L) and ends with a (D). Repeat to make a second 12-square strip-set.

With right sides together, sew one 12-square strip set (L to D) to both the top and bottom of the joined section from #15. Press the seams to one side.

17. With right sides together, sew two 1-1/2" pieced strip-sets together, end-to-end, so they alternate between (L) and (D). Unsew to create a 19-square strip-set that begins and ends with a (D). Repeat to make a second 19-square strip-set that begins and ends with an (L).

With right sides together, sew the first 19-square strip-set that begins and ends with a (D) to the left side of the joined section from #16. Sew the other 19-square strip-set to the other side. Press the seams to one side.

18. Iron an 8-1/2" x 11" piece of Sulky Totally Stable Stabilizer onto the same size piece of silk organza.

19. Print the words (Quaking & Aspen) from the CD in the back of this book.
Place the paper with the words, in the top of an ink-jet copier. Place the silk organza (backed with the Totally Stable), in the paper tray with the Totally Stable side up. Make the copy and then trim, leaving a 1/4" to 1/2" margin around each of the words.

20. Score the back of the Totally Stable with a pin and remove it. Lightly spray KK 2000 onto the wrong side. Position words in place in sections A & G. With a water soluble marker, draw a "box" around the word.

21. Choose the multiple straight stitch. Insert a size 14/90 denim machine needle. Thread the top and bobbin with Sulky 30 wt. Blendables #4044 Butterscotch. Stitch along the drawn lines for the box.

22. Use a straight pin to fray the edges of the silk up to the stitching line and remove the cross threads.

After the Thread-Painted Tree and Leaf are added to the quilt top (see instructions on the following pages):

23. Cut batting and backing fabric to match the size of your finished piece.

24. Lightly spray KK 2000 onto the wrong side of the backing fabric. Smooth the batting over it. Lightly spray KK 2000 onto the wrong side of the pieced wallhanging. Smooth it over the batting. Safety pin the corners and center. Quilt as desired. Square up. Sulky PolyLite 60 wt. Polyester Thread is perfect for hand-sewing the binding.

See more detailed step-by-step "quilting" instructions in the book: *"Quick and Easy Weekend Quilting with Sulky"*

112

Create the Aspen Thread Tree:

Materials for Aspen Tree:

Sulky Stabilizers:
- 1 - 10" square of Sulky Totally Stable Iron-on Stabilizer
- 1 - 10" square of Sulky Soft 'n Sheer Cut-Away Stabilizer

Notions:
- Sulky KK 2000 Temporary Spray Adhesive
- Sulky 30 wt. Cotton Thread Colors #4044 Butterscotch and #1082 Ecru
- 8" Wooden or Spring-tension, Free-motion Embroidery Hoop
- Tree Pattern - on CD in back of this book
- Sharpie™, Extra-fine, Permanent-ink Marker
- 1 - 8" square of Steam-a-Seam Lite®
- Non-stick Pressing Sheet
- Iron and Pressing Pad
- Wood-burning Tool

Sewing Machine with:
- Darning, Spring-loaded Free-motion or Spring-loaded Quilting Foot
- The ability to lower or cover the feed dogs (teeth)
- Size 14/90 Quilting or Topstitch Needle

Fabric Set-up:

1. Secure a piece of Sulky Soft 'n Sheer in the hoop and lay it over the paper tree pattern so the tree is in the center. Trace the pattern with a Sharpie, extra-fine, permanent-ink marker. Unhoop.

2. Use Sulky Soft 'n Sheer because it is light enough to see through and it is strong enough to support the stitches. Plus, if you wish, it can be burned away to create open spaces in the design.

Set up your Machine for Free-Motion Embroidery:

- Drop the feed dogs or cover them
- Attach a Darning, Free-motion, or Quilting Foot (preferably spring loaded)
- On some machines you will need to lower the top tension about one number from normal so the bobbin thread will not be pulled to the top while stitching
- Set the machine for straight stitch (Stitch width on "0")
- Insert a new 14/90 quilting or topstitch needle
- Thread the top and bobbin with Sulky 30 wt. Cotton Blendables Thread #4044 Butterscotch

Thread-Painting Technique:

1. Blendables Threads are ideal for this technique because they have their own built-in mottling due to their short, random color breaks.

2. Start somewhere in the middle of the tree, in the branches close to the trunk. Bring up the bobbin thread through the Soft 'n Sheer by holding the top thread to the back while turning the handwheel toward you through one full stitch, or press the needle-down button twice, if you have one. Hold the top and bobbin thread to the side until you have taken at least 10 stitches, then cut them both close to the fabric.

3. Straight stitch up one of the limbs, all the way to the last leaf. Fill in the small leaves by first outlining them, then fill them by moving the hoop from side-to-side, like building a brick wall. You can also switch your machine to a small zig-zag width of 1.5 to 2mm to do a quick fill-in, like a satin stitch. Since no machine likes to stitch in one place more than a stitch or two, keep your hoop moving as thread will pile up quickly with zig-zag stitching.

4. Follow the pattern to finish each branch with consistent stitches per inch. Straight-stitched lines look nicer if you go over them twice. It's better to sew to the end of the branch and back over it again, rather than to stay and fill in.

> **TIP:** *If you find yourself "painted into a corner", just stitch your way to the outside and go around to the next unfilled area. You can also use the heavier veins in the leaf as highways to get to other sections. The idea is to keep your stitching light. It's okay to have heavier stitching on the thicker branches or the trunk since those are meant to be slightly thicker. Don't worry about being perfect or absolutely straight. Nature isn't perfect.*

Trunk:

1. Thread a new bobbin and the top with Sulky 30 wt. Cotton #1082 Ecru. Use a straight stitch to lightly sew the trunk of the tree. Don't fill in too much because we want to come back in and add some of the Sulky Blendables color for an accent.

2. Thread the top and bobbin with the Sulky 30 wt. Cotton Blendables #4044 Butterscotch and add some bark accents. It's just a hint of extra color.

   Hint: *If you want your tree trunk to look even more realistic, fill the spots on the bark with Sulky 30 wt. Cotton #1005 Black or a dark brown or gray.*

Finishing:

1. For ease of handling, leave the tree in the hoop and use a soldering-iron or wood-burning tool to melt away the Sulky Soft 'n Sheer, right up to the stitches. Start at the center and work your way to the outside. Continue until all of the Soft 'n-Sheer is removed between the branches. Finish by burning away the outside edges.

2. Place the tree, right side down, on a non-stick pressing sheet and iron a piece of Steam-a-Seam Lite onto it. Peel off the release sheet and trim away any excess adhesive, or use the soldering-iron again.

3. Iron a piece of Sulky Totally Stable onto the wrong side of the pieced background (E) where the tree will be placed. *(The Totally Stable provides support for the background fabric and can be removed after the tree is sewn on.)*

4. Place the tree in the center of the right side of block "E". Cover it with a press cloth or a scrap piece of material (to keep the fusible web off your iron) and iron it down.

5. Continue using Sulky 30 wt. Cotton Blendables #4044 Butterscotch to tack down the tree in several places. Sew a straight stitch from the base, running out to the end of a limb, using either free-motion stitches or with the feed dogs up and the regular foot in place.

See more detailed step-by-step "free motion" instructions in the book: ***"Sulky Secrets to Successful Embroidery" Art. #900B-15***

Create the Skeleton Aspen Leaf:

Materials for the Aspen Leaf:

Fabric:
- 1 - 10" square of Bridal Tulle
- 1 - 10" square of a Cotton Cheesecloth that has been tea-dyed overnight

Sulky Stabilizers:
- 1 - 10" square of Sulky Totally Stable Iron-on Stabilizer
- 1 - 10" square of Sulky Fabri-Solvy Water Soluble Stabilizer

Notions:
- Sulky 30 wt. Cotton Blendables™ #4044 Butterscotch or #4040 Biscuit
- 8" Wooden or Spring-tension, Free-motion Embroidery Hoop
- Leaf Pattern - on CD in back of this book
- Water Soluble Marker
- 1 - 8" square of Steam-a-Seam Lite®
- Non-stick Pressing Sheet
- Iron and Pressing Pad
- Wood Burning Tool

Sewing Machine with:
- Darning, Spring-loaded Free-motion or Spring-loaded Quilting Foot
- The ability to lower or cover the feed dogs (teeth)
- Size 14/90 Quilting or Topstitch Needle

Fabric Set-up:

1. Lay a 10" square piece of Sulky Fabri-Solvy over the leaf pattern (found on the CD in the back of this book) and trace it with a water soluble marker. We are using Sulky Fabri-Solvy because it really holds up to heavy stitch penetration and, since we will be able to see both sides, we want all of our stabilizer to disappear.

2. Create a sandwich starting with the 10" square of Tulle on the bottom, then the 10" square of a tea-dyed cheesecloth, and the Sulky Fabri-Solvy with the traced pattern on the top.

3. Place your sandwich on top of the outer ring of your embroidery hoop. Make sure the leaf is positioned in the middle before inserting the inner ring of the hoop.

Set up your Machine for Free-Motion Embroidery:

- Drop the feed dogs or cover them
- Attach a Darning, Free-motion, or Quilting Foot (preferably spring-loaded)
- Set machine for straight stitch (Stitch width on "0")
- Insert a new 14/90 Quilting or Topstitch Needle
- Thread the top and bobbin with Sulky 30 wt. Cotton Blendables Thread #4044 Butterscotch
- On some machines you will need to lower the top tension about one number from normal so the bobbin thread will not be pulled to the top while stitching.

Thread Painting Technique:

1. Blendables® Threads are ideal for this technique because they have their own built-in mottling due to their short, random color breaks.

2. Start somewhere on the outside edge of the leaf and bring up the bobbin thread through the sandwich by holding the top thread to the back while turning the handwheel toward you through one full stitch, or press the needle-down button twice, if you have one.

3. Hold the top and bobbin thread to the side until you have taken at least 10 stitches, then cut them both close to the fabric. Outline the leaf with a straight stitch.

4. Begin to fill the inner part of the leaf by following the water soluble pattern. This is a great time to practice your stippling. The idea is to have consistent stitches per inch. Since no machine likes to stitch in one place more than a stitch or two, keep your hoop moving.

5. Straight lines look best if you go over them twice. It's better to sew to the end of a line, and then sew over it again, rather than to stay and fill in the area.

   When it comes to filling in the leaves, move the hoop from side to side like you are building a brick wall, one row at a time. If you feel this is too slow, you can switch your machine to a medium zig-zag width of 2.5 to 3 mm to do a quick fill in, but continue to move the hoop from side to side so you are filling one row at a time.

> **TIP:** *If you find yourself painted into a corner, just stitch your way to the outside and go around to the next unfilled area. You can also use the heavier veins in the leaf as highways to get to other sections. The idea is to keep your stitching light. It's OK to travel on the thicker veins or outside edges since those are meant to be slightly heavier. Don't worry about being perfect or straight. Nature isn't perfect.*

Stem:

1. Use a straight stitch to sew the stem of the leaf. Finish the stem by setting your zig-zag width just larger than your stitches and satin stitching over them. Tie off with a straight stitch.

2. To add strength and beauty, finish by again going over some of the more prominent veins in the leaf, and go around the outside one more time. You could also go around it with a tiny satin stitch if you really want your leaf edges to stand out.

Finishing:

1. Cut around the leaf, but not too close.

2. Soak the leaf in a bowl of water and rinse after a few minutes.

3. When the leaf is dry, burn away any remaining Tulle and Fabri-Solvy with a wood-burning tool before moving on to the next step.

4. Iron a piece of Sulky Totally Stable to the wrong side of the pieced background (section C) where the leaf will be placed. This will provide support for the base fabric and can be removed after the leaf is sewn on.

5. Pin the leaf in place.

6. Satin stitch over both ends of the stem. This is where your creativity comes in. Rumple the leaf in at least three places and tack it down on one side of the hump with at least 4 to 6 straight stitches. This can be done free-motion or with the feed dogs up and the regular foot in place. This slight wavy look really makes the leaf look real.

The Aspen Tree and Leaf Designs
are also available in the
"Sulky Embroidery
Design Club" as digitized designs.
Visit www.sulky.com for details.

Appliqué Squared

by Joyce Drexler

"This will be one of the most creative appliqué projects that you will ever do. Depending on your color choices and theme, you can create one-of-a-kind looks using some of your favorite fabric. It's easy, fast and fun to do. All you need is a simple decorative stitch on a sewing machine, Sulky Thread and Sulky Stabilizers, a sweatshirt, scraps of fabric and an afternoon.

I know you will love making and sharing these. Simply pick out fabrics and cut squares from them to make a creative grid design. Then, add interest by applying raw-edge-stitched appliqués that coordinate with your sweatshirt colors." --- Joyce

This sweatshirt features Thimbleberries Fabrics.
Always add some squares to the sleeves and back.

117

Materials

- Zig-zag Sewing Machine
- Sulky 30 wt. Rayon, 30 wt. Blendables, and/or Holoshimmer Metallic Embroidery Threads
- Sulky Polyester Invisible Thread in the bobbin
- Size 14/90 Topstitch Needle
- Open-toe Appliqué Foot
- Sulky KK 2000 Temporary Spray Adhesive
- Roll of Sulky Totally Stable™, Tender Touch™ and Soft 'n Sheer™ Stabilizers
- Sulky Iron-on Transfer Pen
- Steam-A-Seam2 Lite™
- An Oversized Sweatshirt
- 4-7 coordinating fabrics and motiffs
- Rotary Cutter, Mat and Quilter's Ruler
- Graph Paper
- Metal Ruler
- General Sewing Supplies

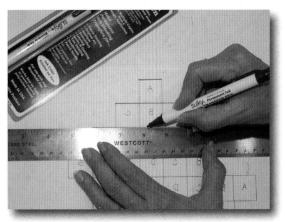

4. Use a metal ruler and draw over the lines with a Sulky Iron-on Transfer Pen that will show well on your sweatshirt color. *A wooden ruler might absorb ink.*

Make the Grid:

Mirror Imaged for transferring, so the letters are reversed. When transferred they will read correctly.

1. Print out the Grid Design from the CD in the back of this book or use a pencil to draw a 1" grid on graph paper.

2. Mark letters to indicate where to place fabrics.

3. To reverse the image, make a copy of the grid design, choosing the mirror image option. The grid can be turned in any direction to best work with your other design details.

5. With a dry iron, press the front of the sweatshirt to preheat the surface.

Lightly spray the right side of the grid pattern with Sulky KK 2000 to help hold it in place. Align the right side of the grid pattern against the front, right side of the sweatshirt.

To achieve a lightly transferred grid design, press and lift the iron after a few seconds; move (do not slide the iron). Repeat until the entire transfer has been pressed before removing the grid pattern. But first, lift one corner to make sure the grid has transferred sufficiently before removing.

118

Cut the Fabrics:

1. Choose high-thread-count fabrics (batiks are perfect) that you wish to use in the grid. Iron Steam-A-Seam2 Lite on the back of the fabrics.

2. Rotary cut the fabric into 1" strips, making sure there is fusible right out to the edges.

3. To keep them from shifting, lightly spray KK 2000 on the wrong side of the strips (Steam-A-Seam side) and lay them on the 1" grid lines on your cutting mat as shown above. Cut them into 1" squares.

4. With the fusible side down, arrange the squares on the sweatshirt grid so that they are butting up against each other. Fuse them in place.

5. If desired, add coordinating appliqués or printed motifs. Rough cut the motif, then apply Steam-a-Seam2 Lite to the wrong side. Cut out the motif. Fuse it to the sweatshirt.

Apply the Stabilizers:

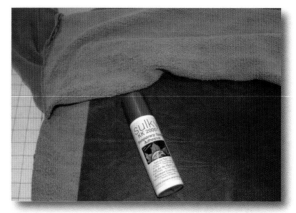

1. Cut open the side seams of the sweatshirt so it will lie flat. Cut a piece of Sulky Soft 'n Sheer Stabilizer (if the sweatshirt is a dark color use black) larger than the area to be stitched; lightly spray it with KK 2000 and smooth it onto the wrong side of the sweatshirt in the area to be stitched. The Soft 'n Sheer will be a permanent stabilizer that will stay on the sweatshirt to stabilize it for sewing as well as through wearing and washing.

2. Cut a piece of Sulky Totally Stable Stabilizer *(or one layer of Tear-Easy could be substituted)* a little larger than the Soft 'n Sheer.

Iron it onto the wrong side of the sweatshirt over the Soft 'n Sheer to give the sweatshirt additional stability while stitching. Afterward, it can be torn away up to the stitching.

Option 1: Set up the Machine for Decorative Stitching:

- Insert a size 14/90 Topstitch Needle
- Wind a Bobbin *slowly with Sulky Clear Polyester Invisible Thread* and put it in the machine
- Thread the top with a Sulky 30 wt. Rayon or 30 wt. Cotton Blendables Thread that coordinates with the grid fabric
- Attach an Open-toe Appliqué Foot and select a decorative stitch like the Feather Stitch

Stitch over the Squares:

1. Following the edges of the squares, stitch over them, alternating direction horizontally and then vertically until all of the raw edges of the squares are stitched.

2. You can also embellish the ribbing by turning 1/2 of the width of the ribbing to the right side and stitching along the edge with a decorative stitch to hold it in place.

Option 2: Set up the Machine for Free-Motion Stitching:

- Attach a Free-Motion Quilting Foot
- Select a Straight Stitch - use Blendables®
- Cover or drop the Feed Teeth

Embellish the Appliqués:

1. Begin free-motion straight stitching 1/8" in from the raw edges, and embellish the inside of the appliqué as much as desired.

2. Remove the Totally Stable or Tear-Easy Stabilizer.

3. To prevent skin irritation from the stitching, iron Sulky Tender Touch over the stitched area on the underside of the sweatshirt.

4. Sew or serge up the side seams. Turn right side out. Press.

Patti Lee created this cute sweatshirt to wear with jeans. She even added a jean's pocket.

120

by Lee Fletcher

Freelance National Educator
Representing Sulky of America

Featuring Sulky® Heat-Away Clear Film™ and Sulky Totally Stable™ Iron-On Stabilizer.

Have you ever wondered how those 3-D fabric appliqués were made that you see on children's wear? Lee will solve the mystery, and you will be dreaming up all kinds of dimensional appliqués for garments, hair bobs, shoes, etc. And, you won't need those annoying 3-D glasses to do it!

Modeled by: Morgyn *(Lee's Granddaughter)*

Materials:

- A purchased outfit with floral designs
- Child's Hat
- Sulky Heat-Away Clear Film Stabilizer
- Sulky Totally Stable Stabilizer
- Sulky 30 wt. Cotton Blendables® Threads to coordinate with the outfit
- Sulky KK 2000™ Temporary Spray Adhesive
- Scraps of fabric or 1/8 yd. for each design element, in a color that coordinates with the outfit's fabrics
- Fusible Web with Release Sheet
- 6" or 8" Free-Motion Spring Tension Embroidery Hoop
- Pencil
- General Sewing Supplies

121

3-D Appliqué

Trace the Flowers & Leaves:

1. Press the outfit. Decide on design elements to copy. For Lee's outfit, she used two different-sized flowers and one leaf. Cut a piece of Sulky Totally Stable large enough on which to copy the designs. Only one of each size flower or leaf needs to be traced.

2. Totally Stable is transparent so you can easily see through it to trace your designs. And, because Totally Stable can be ironed, peeled up, and re-ironed several times, it is an ideal stabilizer to use as a template or pattern.

Lay the shiny side of the stabilizer against the right side of the garment fabric and use an iron (set at the temperature suggested for the receiving fabric) to press the Totally Stable onto the designs to be copied.

Use a pencil to trace one of each of the size flowers or leaves that you want to play with.

Peel the Totally Stable patterns away from the garment. Cut the design template pieces apart and lay them aside for now.

1. Press the shiny side of the Totally Stable patterns onto solid fabrics that match the dress print. Trace around the Totally Stable pattern.

Peel up the Totally Stable pattern and press it onto another area of fabric; trace around it. Repeat until the desired number of design elements are traced. Trace a few extra designs for practice.

Cut the designs out of the fabrics.

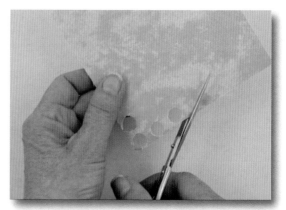

Prepare the Fabrics:

1. Cut a 4-1/2" x 22" piece of each color of fabric. If using scraps, place fabrics wrong sides together.

2. With wrong sides together, fold each fabric strip in half to create 4-1/2" x 11" pieces. Insert a fusible web between each folded fabric and fuse each one together.

2. Iron a fusible web with a release sheet onto the back of the fabric you will use for the flower centers.

Cut enough small circles for each flower and lay them aside for now.

123

Hoop the Flowers:

1. Cut 2 pieces of Sulky Heat-Away Clear Film about 2" larger than the hoop.

2. Lay the outer ring of the hoop on the table. Center one piece of the Heat-Away over it.

3. Holding the can at least 6" away, lightly spray Sulky KK 2000 onto one side of the fabric flowers. With the sticky side down, position the flowers on the Heat-Away in the center of the hoop, far enough away from the edge of the hoop for easy stitching.

4. Lightly spray the tops of the flowers with KK 2000. Center the remaining piece of Heat-Away on top of the flowers. Place the inner hoop inside the outer hoop so that both layers of Heat-Away are taut inside of the hoop.

Set up the Sewing Machine for Appliqué:

1. Insert a new 14/90 embroidery needle and attach an open-toe appliqué foot.

2. Thread the top and bobbin with the same color Sulky 30 wt. Cotton Blendables Thread.

3. Set the machine for a satin stitch with a 2.5 width and a 0.5 length.

4. Select the needle down feature, if available.

5. Adjust the top tension setting as needed to achieve a balanced stitch.

Satin Stitch the Edges:

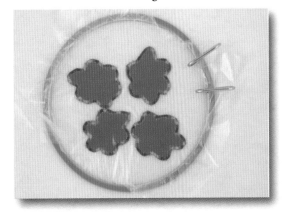

1. Practice stitching on a scrap of fabric first and adjust the tension and stitch settings, if necessary.

2. The thread should completely cover the edge of the practice fabric. Practice stitching around the curves where you will need to pivot to keep the width of the stitch consistant. Stop with the needle down on the widest side of each curve, rotate the flower and continue stitching. Narrow curves may require several rotations to create even stitching. When you are happy with your practice sample, stitch around the outside edges of each flower.

3. Rehoop and change the thread color for each additional design element.

4. Once the stitching is completed, gently tear away the Heat-Away from both sides of the flowers and leaves.

Press to remove any remaining Heat-Away. Use a sticky lint roller to remove any remaining balls of Heat-Away.

124

Prepare the Flower Centers:

1. Center a round flower center over each flower and fuse them into place by removing the release sheet and ironing with steam.

Set up the Machine for Free-Motion Embroidery:

1. Set the machine for straight stitch.
2. Lower the feed teeth or cover them.
3. Attach a darning foot.
4. Thread with a color to coordinate with the center of the flowers.

Position the Flowers and Leaves on the Hat:

1. To attach the Flowers to the Hat, straight stitch in a circular pattern around each flower center.

2. Change the thread to color coordinate with the leaves. Raise the feed teeth. Satin stitch down the center of each leaf to attach it to the hat.

125

Enjoy!

Intro to Embroidery

by Malah Peterson

Freelance National Educator Representing Sulky of America and owner of "A Stitchin' Time" www.a-stitchin.com

In addition to working as a freelance National Sulky Educator for over 16 years, Malah has over 15 years of experience as a professional embroiderer. She has found that there may often be more than one way to stabilize a fabric, depending upon a variety of variables which will be discussed. Some key elements are: Always use a new needle and the smallest hoop possible for the very best results, and never distort or stretch the grain of the fabric being hooped.

Tips to Embroider Knits:

1. *Always do a test stitch-out.*
2. *The most accurate design registration is accomplished by using two layers of Soft 'n Sheer in the hoop and correctly hooping them.*
3. *Spraying Sulky KK 2000 Temporary Spray Adhesive on each layer makes handling them easier.*
4. *For heavier or outerwear garments, try using two layers of Cut-Away Plus if you are stitching a dense design with outlining registration like the sample on the next page. Cut away as much of the stabilizer as possible since using two layers of Cut-Away Plus will make the area relatively stiff.*
5. *Using a Solvy "topper" in most cases will result in a sharper, crisper embroidery.*
6. *When embroidering black outlines and lettering, use Sulky Black Bobbin Thread in the bobbin.*
7. *Cutting away the excess Soft 'n Sheer or Cut-Away Plus results in proper drape and feel of the knit. What remains under the embroidery will aid in retaining the shape of the embroidery through washing and wearing.*

For knits, most embroiderers use permanent "cut-away" stabilizers like Sulky Cut-Away Plus™, Sulky Soft 'n-Sheer™ and the newer Sulky Soft 'n Sheer Extra™ because the stabilizer remains behind the garment and helps to stabilize it through washings and wearings. (You know how embroideries on knits tend to "ball up" after washing? This permanent stabilizer helps to prevent that.)

Sulky Soft 'n Sheer is very soft, soft enough for a baby's skin, and it can be layered in as many layers as the fabric requires. Since some knit fabrics are more stable than others, always do a test on a scrap piece of the fabric, if possible. Once you've gained some experience with this, you will know by feeling and looking at the fabric how much stabilization it will need. Always err on the side of too many layers rather than too few! Or, you can use the newer Sulky *Soft 'n Sheer Extra* which is 1-1/2 times as heavy as the original and has an iron-on backing.

Sulky Cut-Away Plus is a permanent, mid-weight, non-woven stabilizer that is as soft as it is strong. It adds great permanent stability to embroidery, monograms and appliqués on outerwear. Perfect for open-weave fabrics with a complex, high detail or dense design. A wonderful choice for sweatshirts and jackets. Unstable goods require a Cut-Away as do some stable goods onto which a high-stitch-count design will be stitched, but it doesn't always provide a crisp resolution of fine column (satin) stitching like small lettering. You can enhance the clarity and resolution by using Sulky Stiffy Tear-Away as a bottom backing under the hoop (next to the machine) combined with a Cut-Away in the hoop.

Sulky Tender Touch is a permanent, iron-on cover up. You can iron this over the back of the finished embroidery to prevent the stitching from scratching tender skin. A must for children's clothing and anyone with sensitive skin.

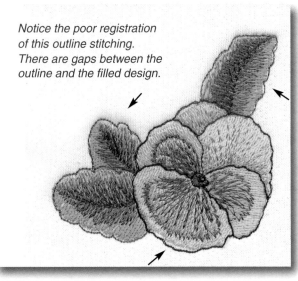

Notice the poor registration of this outline stitching. There are gaps between the outline and the filled design.

Improperly Stabilized Knit:

Wrong: *Only one layer of Sulky Tear-Easy Stabilizer was used. The T-shirt and Tear-Easy were hooped together without using Sulky KK 2000. The white bobbin thread pulled up. Black bobbin thread is a better choice for lettering and outlines.*

One possible better option for knits is to remove the release sheet from *Sulky Sticky+* Tear-Away Stabilizer and adhere it to the bottom of your outer hoop, then gently finger-press your fabric into the Sticky without distorting the weave of the fabric. No need to use the inner hoop. You can spray Sulky KK 2000 onto Sulky Tear-Easy and add as many layers as needed under the Sticky, depending on the weight of the knit. This is ideal when embroidering small "knitted" areas like collars, cuffs, pockets, etc., that aren't large enough to fit into a hoop. The collars, etc., are simply finger-pressed onto the stabilizer.

Or, you can use *Sulky Tear-Easy* in as many layers as necessary (at least three with knits), one hooped with the fabric and 2 under the hoop. Spray KK 2000 on each layer to create a firm "sandwich" of the Tear-Easy, which keeps the needle from "flagging" or pulling up on the layers, resulting in thread breakage and skipped stitches. Professional embroiderers suggest that you layer Tear-Easy in opposite directions. Even though it is non-woven, Tear-Easy does have a definite grain to it. Try tearing a piece from one edge to the other, then try from the opposite sides. One way will tear easier than the other. When you just need strips of Tear-Easy for embroidering edges, etc., you can tear perfectly straight strips, if you tear with the grain. After stitching, gently tear away each layer of Tear-Easy. To prevent harm to the embroidery stitches, always support the stitched area with the fingers of one hand while pulling against the stitching with the other.

Why would you use a Cut-Away Stabilizer instead of a Tear-Away Stabilizer?

When you want the continued support of a stabilizer for the thread area through wearing and laundering, Soft 'n Sheer, Cut-Away Plus, or Soft 'n Sheer Extra are preferred. Tear-aways give temporary support during the embellishing process only. While tear-aways are faster and easier to use, they have limited usefulness on unstable goods because each needle penetration diminishes their support. When a tear-away is perforated, it can be punched out, making it a poor choice for either high stitch count designs, open weave fabrics or lightweight fabrics with a complex design.

How and where do I use Soft 'n Sheer Extra?

Sulky Soft 'n Sheer Extra is 1-1/2 times as heavy as original Soft 'n Sheer with the added convenience of having a fusible, iron-on coating.

This time-saving, mid-weight, cut-away is the perfect choice when you want a cut-away that is a little heavier than Soft 'n Sheer, but not as heavy as Cut-Away Plus. Iron it onto the wrong side of your fabric, using a low temperature of about 260°. This makes it perfect for more delicate fabrics that don't like high heat. On mid-weight knits, use one layer of Soft 'n Sheer Extra rather than two layers of the original Soft 'n Sheer. And since you iron it on, your fabric will not distort when you hoop it.

It is also a wonderful backing for embellishing pillow tops, and as an interfacing in garments that you simply want to remain cool and light. When we don't want fleece or batting in a quilted garment, this is the perfect alternative.

On Pique Polo Shirts or any other kind of knit that has texture such as a Sweater Knit or Thermal Knit . . .

Use a topping of *Sulky Solvy*. This can be hooped with the garment and other stabilizer, or just lightly sprayed with Sulky KK 2000 and smoothed over the top after you have hooped the garment. This method is also recommended when stitching small lettering. It keeps the stitching out on the surface of the garment, rather than letting it sink down into the texture of the garment. *Sulky Soft 'n Sheer Extra* is the perfect iron-on, permanent stabilizer for underneath these kinds of mid-weight knits.

On Sweatshirts or heavier knits . . .

Use *Sulky Cut-Away Plus* to provide extra stabilizing that prevents puckering. Use Solvy as a topping since some heavier knits are often plush enough that some designs can be lost in the depth of the fabric.

Use two layers of *Sulky Soft 'n Sheer or one layer of Sulky Soft 'n Sheer Extra* underneath, and Solvy on top to keep the stitching from getting buried in the nap of the fleece. The only time you may not want to use a cut-away permanent stabilizer on fleece is on fleece blankets that are often reversible. Since blankets don't normally get stretched or stressed like a garment does, you may just want to use one or two layers of *Fabri-Solvy* underneath with Solvy on top. Either, hoop only the stabilizer, spray it lightly with KK 2000, smooth the fleece over it, and add your Solvy topper; or, spray or fuse the stabilizer to the fleece and hoop it along with the Solvy topper. Be aware that some fleece and other napped fabrics will "hoop burn", and the hooped Solvy topper will prevent that as well as enhance the stitch quality.

Stitch out a sample of the design on the same or very similar fabric. This is always very important to do as there may have been a glitch in the electronic transfer of the design to your machine and a color change could be left out or some other error might occur and you don't want to ruin the garment by stitching out an inaccurate design. If, after you stitch out the sample, there is puckering of the fabric, add another layer of stabilizer underneath and re-stitch it. You can either hoop the additional layer or you can slide a layer under the hoop after hooping the other layers.

For lightweight wovens such as lawn, batiste, or handkerchiefs, you will need more stabilizer. Use multiple layers of the lighter *Sulky Tear-Easy* so that when they are carefully torn off, one layer at a time, after the embroidery is complete, less stress is placed on the fabric and embroidery.

Alternate the direction of the layers of Tear-Easy so that the grains cross each other to make the stabilizer stronger and give more stabilization. Spray one layer of Tear-Easy with KK 2000, then place another piece of Tear-Easy on top, with the grain going in the opposite direction. Spray that Tear-Easy with KK 2000 and place the fabric you wish to embroider on top of it, smoothing out all the wrinkles.

Hoop all three layers. Use the basting feature on your machine, if you have it, to help keep all layers secure. If you don't want any residue of stabilizer left on the wrong side of the garment, another option to stabilize lightweight fabric is to use a water soluble stabilizer like *Fabri-Solvy or Ultra Solvy*. When using Fabri-Solvy, hoop both the Fabri-Solvy and fabric. If you are using Ultra Solvy, hoop it, then lightly moisten it with a damp sponge; finger-press the fabric onto the damp Ultra Solvy and smooth out the wrinkles. Let it dry, then stitch your design. After unhooping, cut away the excess Solvy and dissolve what's left by rinsing it out under the faucet.

Heavier-weight wovens (such as denims) need a different approach to stabilizing than you might think. Even though they are a woven fabric, they tend to be somewhat unstable. They tend to stretch as they are being embroidered, and the denser the design, the worse it is. While some people use a tear-away, Malah prefers a permanent cut-away. On shirt-weight denim, she recommends either two layers of *Sulky Soft 'n Sheer*, one layer of *Sulky Soft 'n Sheer Extra*, or one layer of *Sulky Cut-Away Plus*. On heavier denim, you can either use one or two layers of *Sulky Soft 'n Sheer* or *Sulky Totally Stable.* Totally Stable is an iron-on tear-away. Iron the shiny side of Totally Stable onto the wrong side of the fabric with a dry iron. You can also iron multiple layers together to increase the stabilization to keep the denim from stretching while you embroider on it. Then, tear away the excess but save the larger scraps. Usually Totally Stable can be re-ironed up to 7 times with a dry iron.

Topper Tricks

Embroidering on French Terry Cloth Towels using Sulky Super Solvy™ as a "Topper" and Sulky Tear-Easy™ as a support Stabilizer underneath.

On other wovens such as terry cloth, corduroy, etc., use Tear-Easy as the support stabilizer underneath. Place the fabric on top of the Tear-Easy, then place a piece of Super Solvy on top of it, and hoop all three pieces together. Using *Sulky Super Solvy* over toweling or any napped fabric as a "topper" will keep the loops of the terry from poking through the stitching; it also helps prevent stitches from getting lost in the fabric, and it will enhance the clarity of fine lettering and outline stitching.

Unlike tear-away stabilizers, Super Solvy leaves no "fuzzies" or white edges around lettering when removed and adds no bulk to the design. If you are stitching a high-density design, you may want to use more than one layer of Tear-Easy (follow the instructions for lightweight wovens on the previous page).

After the design is stitched, trim all loose threads from both sides before tearing away the Solvy topping. Then spray with water to dissolve the remaining Solvy. Also, tear away the stabilizer from the back. If there are any hoop marks in the fabric, simply spray with fabric sizing and brush the fabric with your hand to raise the nap of the terry cloth.

When you free-motion monogram toweling, you can use the Super Solvy for dual purposes: as a way to get a pattern to follow on top of the toweling; and as a way to hold the loops of the toweling out of the way for better stitch quality.

To trace a pattern onto Super Solvy, lightly spray the Super Solvy with Sulky KK 2000 and

Photo courtesy of Designs in Machine Embroidery Magazine.

smooth it over the pattern sheet to keep it from shifting while tracing. A black, fine-line, permanent-ink marker works well for this technique. However, if you are embroidering with light-colored thread, you may prefer to trace the design with either a water soluble or air soluble marker, or a light-colored, permanent-ink marker so the lines don't show through the white or light colored thread.

Super Solvy allows you to stitch with a delicate straight stitch, or on delicate fabrics, without concern that the stitching will be pulled out or distorted (as in digitized Redwork) when the stabilizer is removed.

Why would you spray KK 2000 on the Super Solvy instead of the toweling?

The toweling would absorb too much of the KK 2000 spray compared to the Super Solvy.

Velvet and Velveteen. . . You need to be aware of the fiber content of the velvet or velveteen. If it is cotton, you can use *Sulky Solvy* as a topper and *Sulky Tear-Easy* for the backing stabilizer. If it is a low-nap velveteen, you may hoop it like corduroy and then, if you have any hoop marks, use fabric sizing to remove them.

Or, you may wish to use *Sulky Sticky+* tear-away stabilizer so you don't leave any hoop marks on the fabric. Cut a piece of Sticky+ about an inch larger than the hoop. Hoop the Sticky+ with the shiny side up (that is the release paper). Score the paper with a straight pin without cutting through the Sticky+. Tear away the paper, exposing the sticky surface of the stabilizer. Place the fabric over the hoop and press it down onto the Sticky+. Lightly spray a piece of Sulky Solvy with KK 2000, smooth it on the top and stitch your design. When finished, gently tear away the Sticky+ from the fabric. Then, tear or cut away the Solvy from the top and spray lightly with water to remove any residue.

Another way to use Sticky+ is to cut a piece of it an inch larger than the hoop, then peel away all of the release paper. Place the outer ring of the hoop onto the sticky surface and attach the hoop onto the machine. Press the fabric onto the sticky surface and stitch the design.

If the velvet is rayon or silk that may water-spot if you get it wet, use *Sulky Heat-Away Clear Film* as a topper. After hooping the Sticky+ and adhering the velvet (following the instructions above), place a piece of Heat-Away on top of the velvet and stitch your design. When finished, gently tear away the Sticky+ from the fabric. Then, tear or cut away the majority of the Heat-Away. Set the temperature on a dry iron according to package directions, and gently touch the iron to the Heat-Away; when little balls are formed, brush them away.

Slippery fabrics like Satin, Taffeta, Silk, etc. . . .
To keep slippery fabrics taut in the hoop, spray Sulky KK 2000 onto *Tear-Easy* and smooth the slippery fabric onto it. Then, hoop both fabrics together. Use the basting feature on your embroidery machine, if available.

Sheer Fabrics like Organdy, Organza, Net, and Tulle . . .
Sandwich sheer fabrics between two layers of either *Sulky Solvy or Super Solvy*. First,

spray one layer with Sulky KK 2000, then place the sheer fabric on top and finger-press them together, smoothing out any wrinkles. Then, spray KK 2000 onto another layer of Solvy or Super Solvy and smooth it on top; hoop all three layers.

After the design is embroidered, remove the "sandwich" from the hoop and press it with a dry iron (set for medium heat) until it is "crispy". (This must be done first in order to quickly dissipate the KK 2000 since it is not water soluble.) Then, place it in a basin of water or rinse it under running water and roll it up in a towel to get rid of the excess water. Allow to air dry or press between two pressing cloths. Another option for dissolving Solvy is to put your item in a lingerie bag and run it through the rinse cycle of your washing machine.

Leather, Vinyl or Faux Leather. . .
Use *Sulky Sticky+* for leather since you don't want to hoop it because that will leave an abrasive hoop mark, which you can't get out with fabric sizing like you can on fabric.

Special Applications

Baseball Caps . . .
present a whole other set of complications when embroidering, but they can be solved if you know how. While some embroidery machines have hoops available to embroider on baseball caps, you can also embroider on them using a regular hoop. Hoop *Sulky Sticky+* using whichever technique you prefer (described earlier in the "Velvet" section). Smooth the front of the cap onto the Sticky+, then center your design and use the trace feature on your machine to get the placement where you want it. Stitch the design, then peel off the cap and remove any excess Sticky+ from around the design. If you like, you can take a scrap of Sticky+ from another project and stick it on the back of the piece just used, so that you don't have to re-hoop the Sticky+ to stitch another design, and you avoid wasting the larger piece of Sticky+.

The above technique can also be used for
dog collars, socks, shirt collars or cuffs, or any small item
that can't be hooped.

Basic Hooping

by Lindee Goodall

Digitizing Expert, Author and former President of Cactus Punch®,
Owner of Lindee G Embroidery

A hoop is necessary to hold the fabric securely during the embroidery process. While fabric may be held in place with adhesive or fusible products for "Hoopless" embroidery, actually placing the fabric between the inner and outer rings of the hoop provides better stability, which means less fabric shifting and slipping, which in turn translates to less design distortion.

For optimum stability, place the fabric between the rings of the hoops whenever possible.

The first step in hooping is determining position and hoop size. It is important to hoop the fabric as straight as possible, with the design as close to the middle as possible, while allowing the fabric to be completely gripped around its perimeter. Always select the smallest hoop that will comfortably accommodate the design. Round hoops generally grip more evenly than rectangular ones. Keeping the design in the center of a small hoop provides more even tensioning of the fabric. Less play in the fabric means more accurate designs. Making sure the fabric is straight allows more precise design placement. It is pretty elementary to move the needle side to side or front to back to get the design centered, but rotating a few degrees requires more skill and is not possible on all machines.

Proper hooping requires an even thickness of fabric and stabilizer around the entire perimeter of the hoop. Extra layers from seams, pockets, or folds in stabilizers prevent even hoop tensions.

Select your Sulky stabilizer backings, toppings and sprays. Your backing, the stabilizer that goes on the bottom, needs to be slightly larger than the hoop so it can be grasped firmly by the hoop, with no edges left out. Smooth your fabric over the backing (a light misting of Sulky KK 2000 can hold the stabilizer in place) and lay it over the loosened outer hoop ring. The outer hoop only needs to be loosened enough to accommodate the fabric, stabilizer, and inner hoop.

*www.sulky.com Jumbo Ferns by
Joyce Drexler for Great Embroidery*

131

If your fabric is wrinkled, it will be harder to hoop smoothly. Press the area to be embroidered before hooping.

Press the inner hoop in place. If the hoop is small enough, simply press the inner hoop straight down. If the hoop is too large for that method, use a rotating, downward motion originating opposite the screw and progressing towards the screw. The screw area is the only place where the outer hoop can expand. If the inner hoop fell in too easily, tighten the screw, remove the fabric, and rehoop. If you have to bounce on the inner hoop to insert it, the screw is too tight and should be loosened a bit. The inner hoop should go in snugly but without undue force.

Once the hoop goes in snugly, check your fabric for wrinkles or puckers. Is the hoop in the correct position? Is your fabric gripped all around the edges? Now turn the hoop over. Is the backing fully hooped? Is it smooth, taut, and wrinkle free? If you see any problems anywhere, rehoop! Minor problems here can become major ones during the embroidery process. If it all looks good, gently push the inner hoop towards the backing so that it slightly extends beyond the outer hoop.

This will add a bit of extra tension to the fabric and keep the hooped goods closer to the throat plate thereby reducing flagging, that unwanted up and down motion of the hoop and/or fabric as the needle moves in and out of the fabric. You are now ready to attach the hoop to your machine.

At this point you may be wondering if I skipped a couple of steps, such as tugging on the fabric and tightening the screw. I did leave them out because they are unnecessary and cause problems. When your fabric is hooped properly, the backing should be taut and the fabric neutral. When you pull on the fabric to "straighten" it, you are stretching it and distorting the grain. If you embroider on stretched fabric, it may look great while it is still in the hoop, but once removed and the fabric relaxes back to its normal state, you will have puckers.

What about tightening the screw? If you hooped snugly as previously indicated, your fabric should be secure. Tightening the screw after hooping does not evenly tighten the hoop; the hoop only becomes tighter at the screw area. And this tightening actually loosens the fabric in this area. To visualize this, imagine what happens when you gather fabric on a thread.

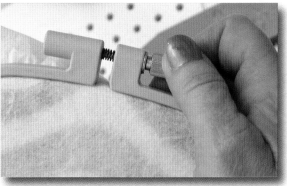
Don't over-tighten the screw.

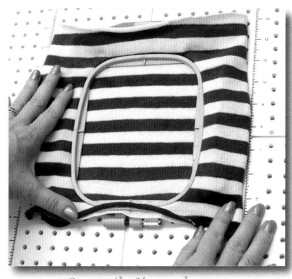
Correctly Hooped.
Grain of knit is straight.

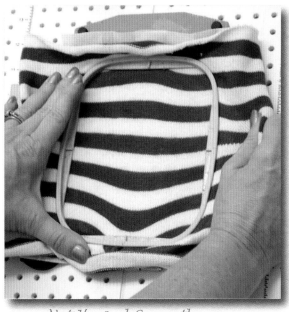
Not Hooped Correctly.
Fabric is distorted.
Grain of knit is not straight. **132**

You are pulling the thread tighter and the fabric is bunching up to form the gathers. The tighter the thread is drawn, the looser the fabric becomes. To see the effects of pulling the fabric and tightening the screw, hoop a piece of striped fabric. A knit will make the distortion even more obvious, but a woven will work as well. First, hoop as previously outlined.

Next, gently run your finger tips over the hooped fabric. Notice the tension of the fabric; it should feel very even. Now, pull on the fabric. Notice that you can't pull the fabric much, if at all, in the corners of the hoop. Inspect the fabric to see where it is now wavy or stretched. Look at the weave of the fabric. Is it still straight? Probably not. Now, run your fingers over the fabric and you will most likely feel areas that are very firm and ones that are soggy. This is what uneven fabric tension feels like. Even fabric tension provides more even embroidery results where outlines are more likely to be in place over the entire design.

How does the fabric feel near the screw? On many rectangular hoops, the screw is in or near the corner, while curves provide the best grip on the fabric. Tighten the screw and then feel the area again. Does it feel more spongy? Once you have the screw set, you do not need to touch it until you change your fabric/stabilizer combination. Simply pop the inner hoop out when embroidery is completed and hoop the next area or piece to be embroidered. Overtightening the screw can damage the fabric and the hoop.

If you have a thin or slippery fabric that needs extra hoop tightness, the answer is to add more fabric between the hoops rather than applying more hoop tension afterwards. I like to use a piece of Sulky Cut-Away stabilizer with the center cut out. This enables me to fill in the space between the hoop rings without adding any bulk to my project since I'm embroidering "in the hole".

Stationary Hooping Aids:

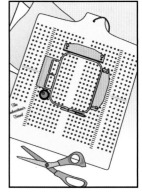

For best results when hooping, I like to use a hooping table, board or other device that will

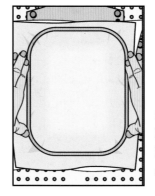

hold the outer hoop in place. No more chasing your outer hoop around while you try to align everything.

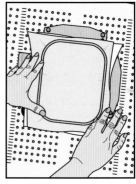

These accessories are particularly useful when hooping garments. Hooping properly and accurately can be time-consuming and difficult. It is definitely not one of the more fun aspects of embroidery, but skimp on this step and you will see it in your final result. Successful embroidery is attention to detail all along the way --- from choosing the right design for your fabric, selecting the most perfect Sulky Threads, using the right needle, and then matching those up with the right combination of Sulky Stabilizers. Hooping is one of the most vital but invisible ingredients in your final masterpiece.

- - - Lindee Goodall

Visit: www.LindeeGEmbroidery.com

Recipes ... for Successful Embroidery

Know what's great about cookbooks? Not only are they full of mouth-watering pictures, but they also contain the specific list of ingredients and complete, step-by-step instructions to help you to successfully create the same wonderful results as the chef who wrote them.

This section is almost the same as your favorite cookbook. It has the most popular fabrics used when embroidering, along with recommendations by nationally-known experts for using professionally recommended Sulky Stabilizers to successfully execute pucker-free embroidery in your own embroidery studio.

So when you are getting ready to embroider that special item for your loved one, check these quick recipes, listed by fabric first, so you can recreate masterful, good-looking, "yummy" results.

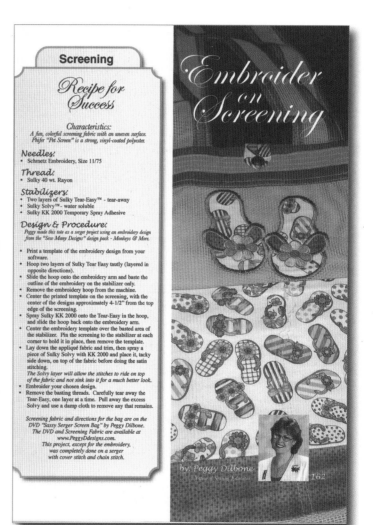

Screening

Recipe for Success

Characteristics:
A fun, colorful screening fabric with an uneven surface. Phifer "Pet Screen" is a strong, vinyl-coated polyester.

Needles:
• Schmetz Embroidery, Size 11/75

Thread:
• Sulky 40 wt. Rayon

Stabilizers:
• Two layers of Sulky Tear-Easy™ - tear-away
• Sulky Solvy™ - water soluble
• Sulky KK 2000 Temporary Spray Adhesive

Design & Procedure:
Peggy made this tote as a serger project using an embroidery design from the "Sew Many Designs" design pack - Monkeys & More.

• Print a template of the embroidery design from your software.
• Hoop two layers of Sulky Tear Easy tautly (layered in opposite directions).
• Slide the hoop onto the embroidery arm and baste the outline of the embroidery on the stabilizer only.
• Remove the embroidery hoop from the machine.
• Center the printed template on the screening, with the center of the designs approximately 4-1/2" from the top edge of the screening.
• Spray Sulky KK 2000 onto the Tear-Easy in the hoop, and slide the hoop back onto the embroidery arm.
• Center the embroidery template over the basted area of the stabilizer. Pin the screening to the stabilizer at each corner to hold it in place, then remove the template.
• Lay down the appliqué fabric and trim, then spray a piece of Sulky Solvy with KK 2000 and place it, tacky side down, on top of the fabric before doing the satin stitching.
The Solvy layer will allow the stitches to ride on top of the fabric and not sink into it for a much better look.
• Embroider your chosen design.
• Remove the basting threads. Carefully tear away the Tear-Easy, one layer at a time. Pull away the excess Solvy and use a damp cloth to remove any that remains.

Screening fabric and directions for the bag are on the DVD "Sassy Serger Screen Bag" by Peggy Dilbone. The DVD and Screening Fabric are available at www.PeggyDdesigns.com. This project, except for the embroidery, was completely done on a serger with cover stitch and chain stitch.

Embroider on Screening

by: Peggy Dilbone
Maker of Sewing Education

162

Grab your Sulky Threads and Stabilizers and start cooking!!!!

A Quick Reference Guide to using Sulky® Threads
for Digitized Embroidery or Free-Motion Work

Type of Sulky Thread	Solid Colors Available	Variegated Available	Multi-Colors Available	Type and Size Needle to use	Spool Pin Vertical	Spool Pin Horizontal	Top Tension	Can be used in the Bobbin	Yardage on Regular Spool	Yardage on King Spool	Yardage on Maxi-Spool	Yardage on Jumbo Cone
30 wt. Rayon	102	36	18	Embroidery/ Topstitch 90 or 100	ok	ok	Loosen Slightly	yes	180	500	N/A	5,500
40 wt. Rayon	333	36	19	Embroidery 80 or 90	ok	ok	Loosen Slightly	yes	250	850	1,500 *in 64 Colors*	5,500
60 wt. *New!* PolyLite™	36	0	24	Embroidery 75	ok	ok	Loosen Slightly	yes	440	N/A	1,500	N/A
40 wt. Poly Deco™	138	0	0	Embroidery 80 or 90	ok	ok	Loosen Slightly	yes	250	900	N/A	5,500
Original Metallic	27	0	9	Metallic or Topstitch 90	ok	ok	Loosen a lot	yes with care	165 *except multi-colors*	1,000 *in 9 Colors*	N/A	5,500 *in 4 Colors*
Sliver™ Metallic	22	0	2	Metallic or Topstitch 90	must	no	Very Loose	yes with care	250	N/A	N/A	N/A
Holoshimmer™ Metallic	22	0	2	Metallic or Topstitch 90	must	no	Very Loose	yes with care	250	N/A	N/A	N/A
30 wt. Cotton/ & Blendables®	66	0	84	Denim or Topstitch 90	ok	ok	Loosen Slightly	yes	N/A	500	N/A	3,200
12 wt. Cotton/ & Blendables®	66	0	84	Denim or Topstitch 90 or 100	ok	ok	Loosen Slightly	yes	N/A	330	N/A	2,100
Polyester Invisible	2	0	0	Embroidery 75, 80 or 90	ok	ok	Loosen Slightly	yes wind slow	440	2,200	N/A	24,600
60 wt. Polyester Bobbin and PolyLite™	2 / 36	0 / 0	0 / 0	N/A / N/A	N/A / N/A	N/A / N/A	N/A / N/A	yes / yes	475 / 440	1,100 / N/A	N/A / 1,500	N/A / N/A

135

Attributes of each type of Sulky Thread and what they are mostly used for.

All are made from the highest quality raw goods available in the world, and they all come on snap-end spools that allow you to store your thread ends neatly.
Flip the snap-end open gently with your thumb.
All are machine Washable, Dryable, and Dry Cleanable.

* Indicates that it is color-fast when washed with detergents that do not contain chlorine or optical brighteners.

---

*✓ Very much the same luster as silk with silk's smoothness, but it is stronger than either silk or cotton thread of the same weight. ✓ Won't fray, fuzz or shrink. ✓ Less stretch than Polyester Thread. ✓ White can be over-dyed. ✓ Perfect for all machine work, sergers, knitting machines and handwork.

Sulky 40 wt. Rayon is the thread most digitizers of computerized embroidery designs use as a standard. Sulky 30 wt. Rayon is 1/3 heavier than 40 wt. and 2/3 heavier than 50 wt. for greater stability, depth and unique color interest in decorative stitching and quilting. Industry experts calculate that one 250 yd. Sulky 40 wt. Rayon spool can create 44,000 embroidery stitches, while an 850 yd. Sulky King spool can create 156,000 stitches, and a 1,500 yd. Maxi-Spool can create 273,000 stitches.

✓ 40 wt. Poly Deco™ is extremely strong and can also be used for general seam sewing. ✓ Both 40 wt. and 60 wt. are trilobal, continuous filament, polyester fibers. They are color-fast when washed with detergents that contain chlorine or optical brighteners, which makes them ideal for sewing and embroidering children's clothing, sports clothes and uniforms. ✓ 60 wt. PolyLite™ is so fine, it is ideal for quilting micro-stippling. ✓ It is also used as colored bobbin thread. ✓ Since it is so thin, a lot can be wound on a bobbin. ✓ Use PolyLite instead of silk thread for invisible, hand-turned appliqués and quilt bindings. ✓ Also used for French Hand Sewing and sewing lingerie. ✓ 60 wt. PolyLite will give the best results when machine or free-motion embroidering small lettering or outlining. ✓ Won't fray, fuzz or shrink.

---

*✓ It is a round, twisted thread of metallic fibers over a strong core. ✓ It does not fuzz, fray or shrink. ✓ Since all Metallics hate abrasion, always use a 14/90 needle, soft pliable stabilizer, and a 60 wt. bobbin thread; sew slower. ✓ Dry at low heat. ✓ Drycleanable.

---

*✓ Both are a thin, flat, ribbon-like polyester film that is metalized with an aluminum layer to give it a brilliant reflectiveness. ✓ Holoshimmer™ is made with a holographic layer and is somewhat stronger than Sliver™. ✓ Does not fuzz, fray or shrink. ✓ Use only on a **vertical spool pin** since it is a flat thread; the twisting action from unwinding off a horizontal spool pin can cause breakage. ✓ When winding onto a bobbin, use a slow speed only. ✓ Always use a 14/90 needle, soft pliable stabilizer, and a 60 wt. bobbin thread; sew slower. ✓ Dry at low heat settings. ✓ Drycleanable. ✓ Do not apply direct heat from an iron. ✓ For craft use, you can curl it by wrapping it around a pencil and heating it.

---

*✓ 2-ply 100% premium long staple Egyptian Cotton. ✓ Matte finish. Solids are perfect to make a country, primitive or antique look. ✓ Blendables® are perfect for machine quilting today's multi-colored, mottled or batik dyed fabrics. ✓ It does fuzz and will shrink slightly. ✓ Very soft feel. ✓ White can be dyed. ✓ Hand embroiderers, punchneedle enthusiasts and hand quilters find it the perfect weight and texture, and prefer it over floss since it come on a convenient spool that will not tangle and does not need to be separated like floss. ✓ Blendables® are multi-colors; 33 of them are subtle and masterful blends of different colors within the same range of tone and intensity. ✓ Randomly change color every 2-1/2" to 5".

✓ It is very fine .004 cross-wound monofilament of 100% Polyester. ✓ Softer, more flexible and more heat tolerant than nylon. ✓ It comes in Smoke and Clear on small or king-size, snap-end spools, or large cones. ✓ Wind on bobbins slowly and not quite full. ✓ Does not fuzz, fray or shrink.

✓ Black and White are lightweight (60 wt.) spun polyester. ✓ Commonly used in the bobbin for digitized computer embroidery. ✓ Won't fuzz, fray or shrink. ✓ PolyLite 60 wt. is made of trilobal, continuous filament, polyester fibers. ✓ The 36 colors of PolyLite are perfect when you want a similar color in the bobbin.

Always do a test.
Stabilizing-At-A-Glance
Computerized Machine Embroidery

This chart contains basic guidelines for your use in building recipes as you take into consideration all fabric, thread and stabilizer used. Make any Sulky Stabilizer (except Ultra Solvy) a "Sticky-type" by spraying it with Sulky KK 2000™ Temporary Spray Adhesive. Solvys can be spritzed with water to make them into a sticky type stabilizer. Always hoop fabric in its relaxed lie. Do not distort the weave or grain when hooping!
* Indicates in the hoop. ** Indicates under the hoop. Use a new needle in size indicated and considering thread used.

Fabric	Needle Size (U) Universal (D) Denim (B) Ballpoint (S) Sharp (L) Leather (T) Topstitch	Backing • or, one layer of Soft 'n Sheer Extra	Topping (O) Original Solvy (S) Super Solvy
Canvas/Denim 10 to 12 oz.	16/100 (D) (U/S)	* 1 layer of Tear-Easy or Stiffy	N/A
Chambray Cotton Shirting	12/80 14/90 (U/S)	* 2 layers of Tear-Easy or Stiffy	N/A
Corduroy	12/80 14/90 (U/S)	* Sticky+	*(O) 1 layer
Cotton/ Quilting weight	12/80 14/90 (U/S)	* Totally Stable & Tear Easy	N/A
Dress Shirt (Poly Blend)	12/80 14/90 (U/S)	* 2 layers of Tear-Easy or Stiffy	N/A
Flannel	12/80 14/90 (U/S)	* 2 layers of Tear-Easy or Stiffy	*(S) 1 layer
Fleece	12/80 14/90 (U/S)	* Sticky+	*(S) 1 layer
Golf Shirt/Pique	12/80 14/90 (B)	* 2 Soft 'n Sheer• or 1 Cut-Away +	*(S) 1 layer
Golf Shirt/Soft Knit	12/80 14/90 (B)	* 2 Soft 'n Sheer• or 1 Cut-Away +	*(S) 1 layer
Hats	14/90 (U/S)	* Sticky+	*(S) 1 layer
Leather (soft)	16/100 (D or L)	* Sticky+ with **2-3 Tear-Easy	N/A
Linen	12/80 14/90 (U/S)	* 1 layer of Tear-Easy or Stiffy	N/A
Lingerie/Silk	12/80 14/90 (U/B)	* Sticky+	N/A
Lycra	11/75 12/80 (U/B)	* 2 Soft 'n Sheer• or 1 Cut-Away +	*(S) 1 layer
Nylon Windbreaker (unlined)	11/75 12/80 (U/S)	* 2 layers of Tear-Easy with ** 1 Tear-Easy	N/A
Satin Jacket (lined)	11/75 12/80 (U/B)	* 2 layers of Tear-Easy	N/A
Satin Jacket (unlined)	11/75 12/80 (U/B)	* Stiffy w/ **2-3 Tear-Easy	N/A
Suiting	11/75 12/80 (U/S)	* 2 Soft 'n Sheer• or 1 Cut-Away +	*(S) 1 layer
Sweater Knit	12/80 14/90 (U/B)	* 2 Cut-Away+ with ** T-E/Stiffy	*(S) 1 layer
Sweatshirt Knit	12/80 14/90 (U/B)	* 2 Cut-Away+ with ** T-E/Stiffy	*(S) 1 layer
T-Shirt Knit	11/75 12/80 (U/B)	* 2 Soft 'n Sheer• with ** 1-2 T-E	*(S) 1 layer
Terry Cloth	12/80 14/90 (U/B)	* 2 layers of Tear-Easy	*(S) 1 layer
Ultra Suede	12/80 14/90 (U/B)	* Sticky+	N/A
Velvet/Velveteen	12/80 (B)	* Sticky+	*Heat-Away
Vinyl	14/90 (D or T)	* 2 layers of Paper Solvy misted with water to act as a sticky stabilizer with vinyl pressed to it.	

Cut Work on Acrylic

by: Christina Dolinar
National Sewing Educator

Featuring:
Sulky Heat-Away
Clear Film

138

Recipe for Success

Characteristics:
A smooth, finely woven fabric that is soft and luxurious.

Needles:
- Schmetz Embroidery, Size 12/80

Thread:
- Sulky 40 wt. Rayon

Stabilizer:
- 2 layers of Sulky Heat-Away™ Clear Film - iron away

This embroidery contains "richelieu" open areas within the design with bars of thread creating little open window panes. Therefore, a stabilizer that would completely disappear after embroidering is essential.

Design & Procedure:
A purchased pashmina-style shawl was chosen to showcase the cut-work embroidery. Fiber care directions state "dry clean only", so a stabilizer that will be completely removed and disappear without water was chosen. The design is very dense, so two layers were needed. The design is from the Husqvarna Viking Majestic Richelieu Collection.

- Hoop two layers of Sulky Heat-Away Clear Film along with the shawl on top.
- Slide the hoop onto the machine. Check the position/placement of the design with templates or the design positioning feature on the machine.
- Embroider. Note: The design first stitches out a running stitch, then the embroidery machine will stop. This is your cue to trim all of the fabric away from INSIDE the running stitch. Remove the hoop from the embroidery arm, and lay it flat on the table. DO NOT REMOVE THE SHAWL FROM THE HOOP. Do not hold the hoop in your lap or in the air as you will loosen the fabric as you trim. Cut away the fabric ONLY from the inside of the stitching. **DO NOT CUT AWAY THE HEAT-AWAY STABILIZER.**
- After trimming, reattach the hoop to the embroidery arm and continue stitching through the design with the color changes as indicated.
- Once the embroidery is complete, remove the shawl from the hoop and trim away large areas of the Heat-Away, being careful not to cut the shawl.
- Place the shawl on your ironing board and set the temperature on a dry iron according to package instructions. Gently touch the iron to the Heat-Away and when little balls are formed, brush them away or use a lint roller to pick up any that remain.

Batiste

Recipe for Success

Characteristics:
A fine, lightweight, sheer, plain-woven, cotton fabric made from various fibers and used especially for French Hand Sewing because of its delicate hand.

Needle:
- Schmetz Universal, size 12/80

Thread:
- Sulky 40 wt. Rayon

Stabilizer:
- Sulky Fabri-Solvy - water soluble

Design & Procedure:
Dress - "Michelle's Madeira Dress" available from: www.thatssewconnie.com

- Hoop with the Fabri-Solvy underneath the fabric and the fabric on top.
- Attach the hoop to the machine. Check the position/ placement of the design with templates or the design positioning feature on the machine.
- Embroider your chosen design.
- When the embroidery is done, soak the fabric in water for up to 30 minutes. Roll the fabric in a towel.
- Let dry and press.
- When pressing, it is important to place your fabric, wrong side up, on a towel or a piece of wool.
- Cut out the pattern pieces. Construct the garment per pattern instructions.

by: *Connie Palmer*
Freelance National
Educator and Designer

139

Open Embroidery

on Boiled Wool

by: Sue
Hausmann

140

Recipe for Success

Characteristics:
A woven or knitted fabric which has been given a coarse, crepe-like texture by heavy felting or by putting it in a high temperature bath.

Needles:
- Schmetz Light Ballpoint Embroidery, Size 14/90

Thread:
- Sulky 40 wt. Rayon #1001 Bright White in the needle
- Sulky White Bobbin Thread in the bobbin

Stabilizers:
- Sulky Solvy™ and Fabri-Solvy™
- Sulky KK 2000™ Temporary Spray Adhesive

Procedure:
This was a purchased boiled wool jacket that was embroidered with a design from the Husqvarna Viking Design Collection - "Black & White Art #205".

- Hoop two layers of Sulky Fabri-Solvy.
- Before putting the hoop on the machine, spray the top layer lightly with Sulky KK 2000 Temporary Spray Adhesive.
- Slide the hoop onto the machine, then place the garment on top of the hoop.
- Check the position/placement of the design with templates or the design positioning feature. The KK 2000 will hold the garment in place, yet allow you to reposition as needed.
- Place a piece of Sulky Solvy on top of the garment and select the "baste in the hoop" option to baste the garment, Fabri-Solvy and Solvy.
- Embroider your chosen design.
- Remove the basting and take the garment out of the hoop. Trim away the excess Fabri-Solvy and Solvy and dissolve away the rest in warm water.

Chambray

Recipe for Success

Presented by Joyce Drexler

Characteristics:
A fine, lightweight fabric woven with white threads across a colored warp. Easy to Embroider.

Needles:
- Schmetz Embroidery, Size 12/80

Thread:
- Beautiful Sulky 40 wt. Rayon

Stabilizer:
- 2 layers of Sulky Tear-Easy™ Stabilizer - tear-away
- Sulky KK 2000™ Temporary Spray Adhesive

Design & Procedure:
Purchased shirt, redesigned. Embroidery Design is from Joyce Drexler's Summer Designer's Collection by Cactus Punch (www.sulky.com). Instructions and other ideas for redesigning shirts can be found in the Sulky Book, "Sulky Secrets to Successful Embroidery", and beginning on page 176 of this book.

- Hoop two layers of Sulky Tear-Easy tautly (layered in opposite directions) and lightly spray the top layer with Sulky KK 2000 before putting the hoop on the machine.
- Slide the hoop onto the embroidery machine, then smooth the shirt on top of the Tear-Easy. Check the position/placement of the design with templates or the design positioning feature on the machine. *The KK 2000 will hold the garment in place, yet allow you to reposition as needed.*
- Once the shirt is positioned, use the "baste in the hoop" option to baste the garment to the hooped Tear-Easy.
- Embroider your chosen design. Joyce's designs can be enlarged up to 20%.
  Tip: Whenever you are embroidering with black thread on top, especially outlining, use a black bobbin thread so you won't have white specks in your embroidery from the bobbin thread being pulled up with a stitch.
- *Note: The fence is a separate appliqué that was fused on with a fusible web, then stitched.*
- Remove the basting. Carefully tear away the excess Tear-Easy, one layer at a time.

Corduroy

Recipe for Success

Characteristics:

A soft, cotton fabric with evenly spaced mini-wales or ridges that give it a raised texture.

Needles:

- Schmetz Topstitch, Size 14/90

Thread:

- Beautiful Sulky 40 wt. Rayon

Stabilizers:

- 2 layers - Sulky Tear-Easy™ Stabilizer - tear away
- 1 layer - Sulky Cut-Away Plus™ - permanent
- 1 layer - Sulky Heat-Away Clear Film™ - iron away
- Sulky KK 2000™ Temporary Spray Adhesive

Design & Procedure:

This was a purchased corduroy shirt that was embroidered with a design by Dakota Collectibles entitled "Golf Scene".

- Lightly spray KK 2000 between two layers of Tear-Easy, then one layer of Cut-Away Plus. Smooth together.
- Secure them in the hoop with the Cut-Away Plus on top. Spray it with KK 2000. Smooth the wrong side of the corduroy shirt over it. *The KK 2000 will hold the corduroy in place, yet allow you to reposition as needed.*
- Spray the right side of the shirt with KK 2000 and smooth a layer of Sulky Heat-Away over it. *The Heat-Away will help the design stitch smoothly on top of the wales of the fabric rather than being distorted by its unevenness.*
- Slide the hoop onto the machine. Check the position/placement of the design with templates or use the design positioning feature on the machine.
- Once the shirt is positioned, use the "baste in the hoop" option to baste the corduroy to the hooped Tear-Easy, Cut-Away Plus and Heat-Away.
- Embroider your chosen design.
- Remove the basting. Trim all the loose threads.
- Tear away the excess Heat-Away. Remove any that is left by ironing with a press cloth. Brush away the little balls of film.
- Carefully tear away the excess Tear-Easy, one layer at a time, while supporting the stitching.
- Cut away the excess Cut-Away Plus.

by Diane
Gloystein
**Freelance National
Educator
Representing
Sulky of America**

Cotton

Recipe for Success

Characteristics:
A soft, staple fabric.

Needles:
• Schmetz Embroidery, Size 14/90 when using Sulky 40 wt. Rayon Threads

Thread:
• The vibrant colors of Sulky 40 wt. Rayon were chosen to bring out the features of each face and coordinate with the fabrics used. The quilting was done in Sulky 40 wt. Multi-colored Rayon thread to add to the graphic nature of the garment.

Stabilizer:
• Totally Stable™ - Black, iron-on, tear-away

Design & Procedure:
Diane constructed this coat, which she calls "Strangers in the Night" (pattern no longer available), and embroidered it with designs from the "Giggles, Gags & Faces" collection designed by Elinor Peace Bailey.

• Stabilize the fabric with Sulky Black Totally Stable by pressing the waxy side of the stabilizer onto the wrong side of the fabric; hoop the stabilized fabric.
• Embroider each face separately.
• Couch raw-edge, ribbon-like yarn around each face.
• Diane carried out the theme onto the lining of the coat where she added the surprise element of embroidered faces peeking out on the black lining, which was also stabilized with Sulky Black Totally Stable.
• Before assembly, carefully tear away the excess stabilizer up to the embroidery.

Visit Diane's website: www.designonawhim.com to see her magnificent Bernina Fashion Show garment which she created with "miles" of painted and dyed Sulky Cut-Away Plus. She then adorned this already magnificent garment with her elegant "fiber bubbles" technique that was featured in the book, ***"Quick & Easy Weekend Quilting with Sulky"***.

Denim

Recipe for Success

Characteristics:
*A coarse, twilled, sturdy cotton cloth.
Very stable and dense with some stretch.*

Presented by Eric Drexler

Needles:
• Schmetz Topstitch, Size 14/90

Thread:
• Sulky Poly Deco Neon Colors - (Black light reflective)
• Sulky Bobbin Thread in the bobbin

Stabilizers:
• Sulky Totally Stable™ - iron-on, tear away, temporary
• Sulky Super Solvy™ - water soluble
• Sulky KK 2000™ Temporary Spray Adhesive

Design & Procedure:
*This was a pair of purchased denim jeans on which Eric
free-motion embroidered the "Hot-Pants"
flames for his daughter, Amber.*

• Use a a black, permanent-ink marker to trace the flame
  design onto Super Solvy from the CD in the back of
  this book.
• Open up the pants leg by seam ripping the serged seam
  up to the knee on one leg and to the crotch on the other.
  This allows you to lay your work flat on the machine
  while embroidering.
• Iron a piece of Sulky Totally Stable onto the wrong side
  of each pant leg that is large enough to cover the area
  under the design.
• Spray Sulky KK 2000 on the right side of the jeans and
  smooth down the Super Solvy (with your traced flame
  design on top of it). If you are matching a design from
  the front of the pants to the back, be sure that it lines
  up.
• Set up the machine for free-motion work.
• Embroider your design using a straight stitch.
• Carefully tear away the excess Super Solvy and Totally
  Stable as you support the stitches with your fingers.
  Use a darning needle or other blunt tool to gently lift
  the Totally Stable out from small areas. Any remaining
  Solvy will wash away.
• Re-sew the legs of the pants.
• *Get hugs from your daughter!!!*

*Variations: Try using Sulky 12 wt. Blendables for a more
  textured look. Increase your needle size to 16/100.
  While the pants are flat, you could also add some beads,
  an applique or even cut-work. It's fun and very unique.*

144

by: Sue Hausmann

145

Dbl. Faced Wool

Recipe for Success

Characteristics:

Needles:
• Schmetz Embroidery, Size 14/90

Thread:
• Sulky 40 wt. Rayon

Stabilizer:
• 2 layers of Sulky Tear-Easy - tear-away
• Sulky KK 2000 Temporary Spray Adhesive

Design & Procedure:
This was a purchased jacket with embroidery from the Husqvarna Viking Design Collection "Colors of Autumn #153".

• Hoop two layers of Sulky Tear-Easy tautly (layered in opposite directions) and lightly spray the top layer with Sulky KK 2000 before putting the hoop on the embroidery machine.
• Slide the hoop onto the machine, then place the garment on top of the hoop. Check the position/placement of the design with templates or the design positioning feature on the machine. The KK 2000 will hold the garment in place, yet allow you to reposition as needed.
• Once the garment is positioned, use the "baste in the hoop" option to baste the garment to the hooped Tear-Easy.
• Embroider your chosen design.
• Remove the basting.
• Carefully tear away the Tear-Easy, one layer at a time.

by: Eileen Roche
and Tamara Evans   146

Double-Knit Poly

Recipe for Success

Characteristics:
A knit fabric similar to jersey that is made with two sets of needles producing a double thickness joined by interlocking stitches.

Needle:
• Schmetz Light Ball-Point Embroidery, Size 14/90

Thread:
• Sulky 40 wt. Rayon Thread

Stabilizers:
• Sulky Soft 'n Sheer™ or Soft 'n Sheer Extra - permanent
• Sulky Tear-Easy™ - tear-away
• Sulky Solvy™ - water soluble
• Sulky KK 2000™ Temporary Spray Adhesive

Design & Procedure:
Amazing Designs Fashion Embellishments II (ADP-29JD) design #ADP-29JEREMB211, as seen on the cover of **Designs in Machine Embroidery** *Magazine.*

In Embroidery Editing Software, remove colors #1 and 2, the leaf and stem. Save the design under a new name and print a template of the edited design. Remove some of the petals to add interest to the repeated design and save this design under a different name. Print a template of the design.

• Cut out the front bodice pattern pieces from your fabric and sew the shoulder seams. Place the bodice on a dress form and audition the printed embroidery templates on the garment.
• Once your layout is arranged, hoop the garment with Sulky Soft 'n Sheer or Soft 'n Sheer Extra.
• Position the needle over the template, remove the template and lightly spray the fabric with Sulky KK-2000 Temporary Spray Adhesive.
• Smooth a layer of Sulky Solvy over the design area to keep the stitching from being lost in the knit.
• Embroider each flower.
• Switch to regular sewing and select a satin stitch with a 3.0 width and a 0.3 length.
• Slide Sulky Tear-Easy under the stitching area to keep the fabric from tunneling as you stitch a long stem on each flower, sewing right off the edge of the garment.
• Satin Stitch the stems.
• Carefully remove the excess stabilizer.
• Construct the tunic.

Faux Fur

Recipe for Success

Characteristics:
"Faux fur" designates any synthetic material (usually polyester or acrylic) which mimics the appearance and feel of real fur, without the use of animal products.

Needles:
- Schmetz Embroidery, Size 14/90

Thread:
- Sulky Top Quality 40 wt. Rayon

Stabilizers:
- Sulky Solvy™ - water soluble
- 2 layers of Tear-Easy™ - tear-away, temporary
- Sulky KK 2000™ Temporary Spray Adhesive

Design & Procedure:
The rug has a fabric backing. The design is from Planet Applique, www.planetapplique.com and is titled, "Bella Frame Applique". Instead of fabric, as suggested for the applique, Alyson used a "lay down" stitch pattern. Then she monogrammed the initials directly over it. Always choose a bold design for faux fur.

- Hoop 2 layers of Sulky Tear-Easy (layered in opposite directions). Spray the top layer with Sulky KK 2000 so the surface is tacky.
- Slide the hoop onto the machine.
- Smooth the wrong side of the fur rug onto the Sulky Tear-Easy.
- Check the position/placement of the design with templates or the design positioning feature on the machine. The KK 2000 will hold the rug in place, yet allow you to reposition as needed.
- Once the rug is positioned, place a layer of Sulky Solvy on top, then use the "baste in the hoop" option to baste everything together. The Solvy layer will allow the stitches to ride on top of the fabric and not sink into it, as well as hold the fur down for a much neater look.
- Roll up the sides of the rug. If it has any weight to it, you may need to support it by keeping your hands under the excess so it doesn't pull down.
- Embroider your chosen design.
- Remove the basting, remove the Solvy, and tear away the excess Tear-Easy, one layer at a time.
- You may need to trim away some of the fur from the design with sharp, short-bladed scissors.

Embroidered on a professional embroidery machine by:
Alyson Prater for her daughter, Isabelle Prater
Action Embroidery
Cartersville, GA 30120

Flannel

Recipe for Success

Characteristics:
A fuzzy, soft, warm, durable woven fabric that can be dyed or printed.

Needle:
• Schmetz Topstitch, Size 14/90

Thread:
Beautiful Sulky 40 wt. Rayon

Stabilizers:
• 1 layer - Sulky Tear-Easy™ Stabilizer - tear away
• 1 layer - Sulky Cut-Away Plus™ - permanent
• 1 layer - Sulky Solvy™ - water soluble
• Sulky KK 2000™ Temporary Spray Adhesive

Design & Procedure:
This was a purchased flannel shirt that we embroidered with a design by Dakota Collectibles entitled "Golf Scene".

• Lightly spray KK 2000 Temporary Spray Adhesive between a layer of Tear-Easy and a layer of Cut-Away Plus. Smooth them together.
• Secure them in the hoop with the Cut-Away Plus facing up. Spray it with KK 2000. Smooth the flannel over it. *The KK 2000 will hold the flannel in place, yet allow you to reposition as needed.*
• Spray the top of the flannel and smooth a layer of Sulky Solvy over it. *The Solvy will help the stitching to float on top of the fabric rather than allow small stitching to get lost in the softness of the fabric.*
• Slide the hoop onto the machine. Check the position/placement of the design with templates or use the design positioning feature on the machine.
• Once the flannel is positioned, use the "baste in the hoop" option to baste the flannel to the hooped Tear-Easy, Cut-Away Plus and Solvy.
• Embroider your chosen design.
• Remove the basting. Trim all the loose threads.
• Tear away the excess Solvy. Remove any that is left with a damp sponge.
• Tear away the excess Tear-Easy while supporting the stitching.
• Cut away the excess Cut-Away Plus.
• If needed, press the embroidered area, right side down, on a soft towel.

148

Thread Sketching

by: Sue Hausmann

Recipe for Success

Characteristics:

A light, sheer, open-weave fabric made of cotton or silk.

Needle:
- Schmetz Embroidery, Size 12/80

Thread:
- Generally, for digitized embroidery designs, soft and warm-looking Sulky 40 wt. Rayon is the preferred thread. Use Sulky Bobbin Thread in the bobbin.

Stabilizers:
- Sulky Tender Touch™ - iron-on, permanent
- Sulky Tear-Easy™ - tear-away, temporary
- Sulky Solvy™ - water soluble
- Sulky KK 2000™ Temporary Spray Adhesive

Design & Procedure:
This was a purchased, off-white jacket that came with rayon stipple quilting already on it. We embroidered it with a Grand Dream Hoop design from the Pfaff Creative Vision Collection.

- In the area to be embroidered, fuse Sulky Tender Touch onto the wrong side of the jacket. Put the maximum stretch of the Tender Touch lengthwise on the garment and give the Tender Touch a "blast of steam" to shrink it before fusing. Don't worry about the size of the Tender Touch being larger than the design because you will pull it up and trim away the excess after embroidering. To make it easier to pull up, do not "over fuse" it.
- Hoop two layers of Tear-Easy tautly (stacked in opposite directions) and spray the top one with Sulky KK-2000 Temporary Spray Adhesive before putting the hoop on the machine.
- Position the jacket on top of the hoop. Check the position/placement. The KK 2000 will hold the garment in place, yet allow you to reposition as needed.
- Once the garment is positioned, place a piece of Sulky Solvy on top.
- Use the "baste-in-the-hoop" feature.
- Embroider your chosen design.
- Once embroidered, remove the basting and excess Solvy, and carefully tear away the Tear-Easy, one layer at a time.
- Pull the excess Tender Touch away from the wrong side of the garment around the outside of the design and trim it away with a blunt-tip, bent trimming scissors.

Handkerchief Linen

Embroider on Linen

by: Hope Yoder

Recipe for Success

Characteristics:
A woven fabric made from natural fibers taken from the stalk of the flax plant. Does not stretch and is easy to embroider by hand or machine.

Needles:
- Schmetz Microtex, size 12/80

Thread:
- Sulky 40 wt. Rayon

Stabilizer:
- Sulky Fabri-Solvy™
- Sulky KK 2000™ Temporary Spray Adhesive

Design & Procedure:
Embroidery designs are from the "Heirloom Embellishments Volume 3 - Lace Shaping" Collection available at: www.hopeyoder.com. This one only works with English cotton netting. Nylon tulle will stretch and cause the foundation fabric to tear away from the stitches.

- Dip the cotton netting in hot water and wring out the excess water. Dip the netting into straight liquid starch, remove it and lay it flat. When the netting is almost dry, iron it flat to remove any wrinkles.
- Hoop the linen together with Sulky Fabri-Solvy on top.
- Spray the starched cotton netting with Sulky KK 2000 and lay a large piece on top of the hoop; finger-press the netting to the stabilizer.
- Embroider the first color, which is an outline of the heart. Carefully trim away the excess netting outside of the heart, leaving a narrow band of netting.
- Embroider the next color, which is a reinforced zig-zag stitch, following the same path as the first color. Remove the hoop from the embroidery arm and turn it over. From the wrong side, carefully trim away the linen that is inside the heart-shaped stitching lines. As you cut away the linen you will have a barrier (Fabri-Solvy) which will protect the delicate cotton netting from accidentally being cut. After trimming, float a piece of Fabri-Solvy underneath the hoop and stitch the dainty stitches inside the netting that give the design the appearance of lace.
- When your embroidery is complete, soak the fabric in water for up to 30 minutes, then wring out the excess water by rolling the fabric in a bath towel. It is not necessary to remove all of the Fabri-Solvy from the fabric as it will help stabilize the fabric, making the finished project nice and crisp.

150

Lycra/Spandex

Recipe for Success

Characteristics:
Lightweight and very stretchy

Needles:
- Schmetz Universal or Stretch, Size 12/80

Thread:
- Top Quality Sulky 40 wt. Rayon

Stabilizer:
- 3 layers of Sulky Soft 'n Sheer™ - permanent, cut-away
- Sulky KK 2000™ Temporary Spray Adhesive

Design & Procedure:

This Devil Stingray Gymnastics design was custom digitized by Jason Prater's Dad for his Granddaughter's Gymnastic's group. The design has 10,000 stitches.

- Cut 3 pieces of Sulky Soft 'n Sheer larger than the hoop.
- Spray each piece with Sulky KK 2000 and layer them all together.
- Cut open the side seam of the leotard and fold it back.
- Spray the top layer of the Soft 'n Sheer with KK 2000 to make it tacky.
- Slightly stretch the leotard fabric as you smooth it onto the Soft 'n Sheer.
- Hoop all together. Sometimes it's easier when you have an extra hand to help you hoop a stretchy fabric.
- Slide the hoop onto the machine. Check the position/ placement of the design with templates or the design positioning feature on the machine.
- Once the garment is positioned, use the "baste in the hoop" option to baste the garment to the hooped Soft 'n Sheer.
- Embroider your chosen design.
- Remove the basting stitches and the jump stitches from the front, and the loose bobbin threads from the back. Cut away the excess Soft 'n Sheer from around the design with a blunt-end scissors.
- The Soft 'n Sheer has a soft feel and does not make the embroidery stiff.

Embroidered by Alyson Prater for her daughter, Abigail.

Nylon Windbreaker

Recipe for Success

Characteristics:
Slick, smooth, densely woven surface.

Needles:
- Schmetz Embroidery, Size 14/90

Thread:
- Top Quality Sulky 40 wt. Rayon

Stabilizer:
- 2 layers of Sulky Tear-Easy™ - tear-away, temporary
- Sulky KK 2000™ Temporary Spray Adhesive

Design & Procedure:
A breast cancer design from The Dolly Lama Collection "Fight for a Cure" by Embroidables www.embroidables.com.

- Lightly spray a layer of Sulky Tear-Easy Stabilizer with Sulky KK 2000 and smooth another layer over it in the opposite direction. Secure in the hoop.
- Spray the top layer with KK 2000.
- Slide the hoop onto the machine.
- Smooth the windbreaker in position over the Tear-Easy Stabilizer.
- Check the position/placement of the design with templates or the design positioning feature on the machine.
- Use the "baste in the hoop" option to baste the windbreaker to the Tear-Easy.
- Embroider your chosen design.
- Remove the basting stitches and clip all of the loose threads from the back and front.
- Carefully tear away the Tear-Easy Stabilizer, one layer at a time.

For a free breast cancer support embroidery design, see the CD in the back of this book. www.stitchingforpink.org

Embroidered on a professional embroidery machine by:

Alyson Prater
Action Embroidery
Cartersville, GA 30120
770-387-9066

Open-Crochet Knit

Recipe for Success

Characteristics:
A medium-weight, crocheted fabric that has a resonable amount of stretch and texture to it.

Needles:
- Schmetz Embroidery, Size 14/90

Thread:
- Sulky 40 wt. Rayon Thread.

Stabilizers:
- Sulky Solvy™ - water soluble
- Sulky Sticky+™ - temporary, cut-away
- Sulky KK 2000™ Temporary Spray Adhesive

Design & Procedure:
This was a purchased, knitted hat that was embroidered with a Tahoka Daisy from www.emblibrary.com.

- Hoop a piece of Sulky Sticky+ and use a pin to score an "X" in the release sheet. Pull the release sheet up and tear it away.
- Smooth the wrong side of the knitted hat onto the Sticky+. Pin the rest of the hat out of the way.
- Slide the hoop onto the machine.
- Check the position/placement of the design with templates or the design positioning feature on the machine. Reposition on the Sticky+ as needed.
- Once the garment is positioned, lightly spray KK 2000 onto a layer of Sulky Solvy and position it on top, then use the "baste in the hoop" option to baste the hat to the hooped Sticky+, and help hold the Solvy in place on top. The Solvy layer will allow the stitches to ride on top of the fabric and not sink into it for a much prettier look.
- Embroider your chosen design.
- Remove the embroidery from the hoop, and remove the basting stitches and the excess Solvy and Sticky+.

Embroidered on a professional embroidery machine by:

Alyson Prater
Action Embroidery
Cartersville, GA 30120
770-387-9066

Made for her daughter, Abigail (photo). The design had almost 15,000 stitches.

153

Organza

Recipe for Success

Characteristics:
A thin, woven, sheer fabric originally made from silk, but today it is often polyester or nylon. The most luxurious organzas are still silk.

Needles:
• Schmetz Embroidery, Size 12/80

Thread:
• Use the same Sulky 40 wt. Rayon in both the bobbin and on the top

Stabilizer:
• Sulky Ultra Solvy™ - water soluble

Design & Procedure:
The organza was embroidered using the Husqvarna Viking Majestic Cutwork Collection, and then applied to the T-shirt.

• Hoop black organza alone with Sulky Ultra Solvy underneath.
• Stitch out the leaves and flowers with Sulky 40 wt. Rayon Thread #1005 Black, or embroider your chosen design.
• Once embroidered, remove the fabric from the hoop and carefully trim away any excess Ultra Solvy.
• Agitate in water to dissolve away the Ultra Solvy that was incorporated into the embroidery. After the embroidery is dry, use a stencil-burning tool to burn away the designs out of the organza.
• Arrange the embroidered organza around the neckline of the T-shirt and stitch it down with a straight stitch following the satin-stitched edge of some of the petals, but not on the very edge of the flower. On the leaves, only stitch down the center vein.

"I was inspired to create this project by seeing a very expensive Vera Wang T-shirt that had dimensional flowers all around the neckline." - Chris

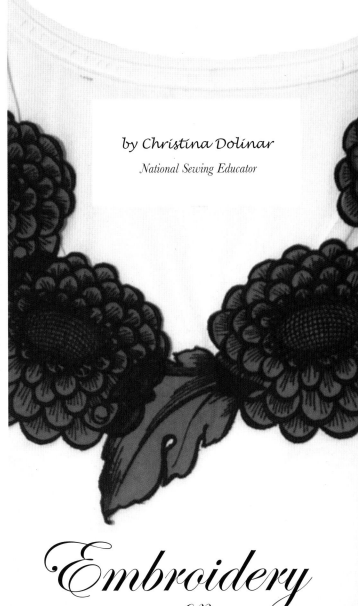

by Christina Dolinar

National Sewing Educator

Embroidery on Organza

then applied to a T-Shirt

154

Piqué Knit

Recipe for Success

Characteristics:
A knit fabric with raised, lengthwise "cords" which are part of the weave that gives it a textured finish.

Needles:
• Schmetz Ballpoint, Size 14/90

Thread:
• Top Quality Sulky 40 wt. Rayon

Stabilizers:
• Sulky Solvy™ - water soluble
• Sulky Soft 'n Sheer Extra™ - cut-away, permanent
• Sulky Black Tear-Easy™ - tear-away, temporary
• Sulky KK 2000™ Temporary Spray Adhesive

Design & Procedure:
This was a purchased, polo-style shirt that was embroidered with the Sulky of America Logo which had 7,500 stitches.

• Hoop a layer of Sulky Soft 'n Sheer Extra; lightly spray it with Sulky KK 2000 so the surface is tacky.
• Slide the hoop onto the machine.
• Smooth the wrong side of the shirt onto the stabilizer. Pin the rest of the shirt out of the way.
• Check the position/placement of the design with templates or the design positioning feature on the machine. The KK 2000 will hold the shirt in place, yet allow you to reposition as needed.
• Once the garment is positioned, slide a piece of Sulky Tear-Easy under it and place a layer of Sulky Solvy on top, then use the "baste in the hoop" option to baste everything together. The Solvy layer will allow the stitches to ride on top of the uneven surface of the knit fabric and not sink into it for a much better look.
• Embroider your chosen design.
• Remove the basting stitches and clip all of the loose threads from the back and front.
• Carefully tear away the excess Solvy and Tear-Easy. Cut away the excess Soft 'n Sheer Extra with a blunt-tip, bent scissors 1/4" away from the stitching.

155

Modeled by: Jason Prater, President of Sulky of America

Express yourself with...
sulky®
Decorative Thread,
Stabilizers & Books

Embroidered on a professional embroidery machine by:

Alyson Prater
Action Embroidery
Cartersville, GA 30120
770-387-9066

Polar Fleece

Recipe for Success

Characteristics:
Polartex 200® - A soft, fuzzy, cushy, man-made fiber.

Needles:
- Schmetz Embroidery, Size 12/80

Thread:
- Sulky 40 wt. Rayon

Stabilizers:
- Sulky Cut-Away Plus™ - cut-away, permanent
- Sulky Fabri-Solvy™ (or Super Solvy™) - water soluble
- Sulky KK 2000™ Temporary Spray Adhesive

Design & Procedure:
The V-Neck Hooded Pullover is from the **Ultimate Polarfleece® Pizzazz** book by Pattie Otto. The hood and pockets are trimmed with 4 strands each of the 4 main colors of Sulky 40 wt. Rayon used in the embroideries, held as one, and crocheted around the edges through the holes created by the Edge Perfect Blade™. The designs are from the "Mola • Mola • Mola" design pack by Great Copy Patterns.

- Before constructing, mark the center front, center back and center of the left sleeve with chalk or a fabric marker. Create a paper or stitched template of each design and use them for design placement. Mark the center of each design on the right side of the fabric.
- Cut a piece of Sulky Cut-Away Plus larger than the hoop and hoop it firmly. Lightly spray Sulky KK-2000 onto the Cut-Away Plus. With the right side of the Polartec fleece up, center the fabric in the hoop and gently finger-press the fabric onto the stabilizer.
- Cut a piece of Sulky Fabri-Solvy larger than the design. To prevent the stitches from sinking into the fabric, place the Fabri-Solvy over the Polartec in the hoop.
- Place the hoop in the machine. Use the "baste in the hoop" option to hold the Fabri-Solvy in place while embroidering.
- Embroider your chosen design. Remove the hoop from the machine. Trim the Cut-Away Plus, being careful not to cut the stitching or the fabric.
- Trim the Fabri-Solvy close to the embroidery. Repeat for the remaining designs.
- Construct the pullover as the pattern directs. Remove the remaining Fabri-Solvy by rinsing the pullover in luke-warm water; line dry.
- To embroider these designs on a ready-to-wear pullover, for easier access, use a seam ripper to open the side/underarm seam.

Hooping Tip: *Polartec and other lofty fabrics should not be hooped. The pressure of the hoop will cause hoop-burn on the thick fabric. Instead, use Sulky Cut-Away Plus along with Sulky KK 2000, or Sulky Sticky+. Also, since fabrics like Polartec stretch easily, a permanent cut-away stabilizer like Cut-Away Plus is needed to keep the fabric from puckering during use.*

by: *Pattie Otto*
Owner, Designer
Great Copy Pattern Co.
www.greatcopy.com

156

Eric Drexler - National Sulky Educator

Monogram a Cuff...

on a long sleeve dress shirt by using **Sulky Sticky+** Stabilizer secured in the hoop. Score the inside area of the release sheet and peel it away. Stick the opened cuff onto the Sticky+ Stabilizer. Place the hoop on the machine. Slide a sheet of Tear-Easy under the hoop. Position and embroider. Remove the excess stabilizer.

Poplin Shirting

Recipe for Success

Characteristics:
A soft, thin, stable, woven fabric.

Needles:
• Schmetz Embroidery, Size 12/80

Thread:
• The vibrant, shiny colors of Sulky 40 wt. Rayon

Stabilizers:
• Sulky Soft 'n Sheer Extra™ - iron-on, permanent
• 2 layers of Sulky Tear Easy™ - tear-away
• Sulky KK 2000™ Temporary Spray Adhesive

Design & Procedure:
Logo shirts are used in just about every business these days. If you have a small business or club and need to embroider shirts for them, this recipe will certainly come in handy.

• Lightly spray one layer of Sulky Tear-Easy with Sulky KK 2000, then smooth another layer over it. Hoop.
• Iron the fusible side of Sulky Soft 'n Sheer Extra onto the wrong side of the shirt in the area to be embroidered.
• Spray the hooped Tear-Easy with KK 2000 to give it a tacky surface. Position the shirt, right side up over the Tear-Easy and smooth in place. *The KK 2000 allows you to reposition, if needed.*
• Place the hoop on the arm of the embroidery machine. Use the "Baste" or "Fix" feature to hold all the layers together.
• Embroider your chosen design while keeping the rest of the shirt out of the way.
• Clip all of the loose threads from the back and the jump stitches from the front.
• Carefully remove the excess Tear-Easy, one layer at a time, while supporting the stitching.

Soft 'n Sheer Extra keeps the fabric of the shirt from creeping while being embroidered, and remains to help support the embroidery through laundering. If needed, always press your embroidery from the wrong side of the fabric, face down on a soft towel.

Quilted Silk Dupioni

Recipe for Success

Characteristics:

A shimmering silk that is created by weaving silk threads of two different colors into a weave that seems to change colors as the silk is moved around in different lights. It also resists wrinkles and is totally reversible.

Needles:
- Schmetz Microtex, Size 12/80

Thread:
- Sulky 40 wt. Rayon

Stabilizers:
- Sulky Tender Touch™ - iron-on, permanent
- Sulky Tear-Easy™ - tear-away, temporary

Design & Procedure:

The challenge you face in creating a quilted silk dupioni jacket lies in the sleeves because they are not lined with fusible fleece. The front and back of the jacket are lined with a very lightweight fusible fleece, then cross-hatched using a Sulky 40 wt. Rayon Thread and a guide-bar spaced 2" away from the center needle position. The embroidery design is from "Heirloom Embellishments Volume 4 - English Lace Ovals" which is available at www.hopeyoder.com.

- Cut a piece of fabric several inches larger than the sleeve pattern pieces. Use a press cloth to iron Sulky Tender Touch onto the wrong side of the sleeve fabric.
- Shape a lace bow over each sleeve and topstitch the bow using a Sulky 40 wt. Rayon Thread that matches the lace.
- Fuse the fleece onto the back of the jacket; quilt.
- Prep the back of the fabric by ironing Sulky Tender Touch onto the wrong side of it to add stability and help eliminate the possibility of the quilting lines showing through once the embroidery is completed.
- Hoop the quilted fabric, then slide one layer of Sulky Tear-Easy underneath; embroider your chosen design.
- Carefully remove the Tear-Easy.
- Stabilize and embroider the heart embroidery on the front in the same manner.

Silk Dupioni

by: Hope Yoder
*Nationally known
Author, Designer, and Educator*
www.hopeyoder.com

158

Raw Edge Appliqué

on Raw Silk

by: Sue Hausmann

Raw Silk

Recipe for Success

Characteristics:
Raw Silk fabric is made from fibers that have been degummed and taken off the silk cocoon, but not spun yet. It tends to be a medium weight fabric that is loosely woven with a textured surface.

Needle:
- Schmetz Light Ballpoint Embroidery, size 14/90

Thread:
- Sulky 40 wt. Rayon

Stabilizers:
- Sulky Tender Touch™ - iron-on, permanent
- Sulky Tear-Easy™ - tear-away, temporary
- Sulky KK 2000™ Temporary Spray Adhesive

Design & Procedure:
This was a purchased, pink, raw silk, tweed jacket that was embroidered with a design from the Husqvarna Viking Design Collection, #162 Blooming Flowers, featuring raw edge appliqué.

- Use a seam ripper to open the front lining to the facing seam; fold and tape the lining out of the way so that you can embroider through the jacket fabric only.
- To stabilize the loosely woven fabric of the jacket, before hooping the jacket, fuse Sulky Tender Touch to the wrong side of it in the area to be embroidered. Don't worry about the size of the Tender Touch being larger than the embroidery design, as you will trim the excess away after embroidering. To make it easier to pull up later, do not "over fuse" it.
- Hoop two layers of Sulky Tear-Easy tautly (layered in opposite directions) and lightly spray the top layer with Sulky KK 2000 before putting the hoop on the embroidery machine.
- Slide the hoop onto the machine, then place the garment on top of the hoop. Check the position/placement of the design with templates or the design positioning feature on the machine. The KK 2000 will hold the garment in place, yet allow repositioning as needed.
- Once the garment is positioned, use the "baste-in-the-hoop" option to baste the garment to the hooped Tear-Easy.
- Embroider following the instructions for placement of appliqué fabric. Spray KK 2000 on the wrong side of the fabrics. Once the appliqué stitching is completed, trim the appliqué fabric to 1/8" outside the stitching.
- Remove the basting and tear away the Tear-Easy, one layer at a time. Pull the excess Tender Touch from around the design and trim it away using a blunt-tipped scissors.

Rib Knit

Recipe for Success

Characteristics:
Very stretchy and soft.

Needles:
• Schmetz Embroidery, Size 12/80

Thread:
• Sulky 40 wt. Rayon

Stabilizers:
• Sulky Soft 'n Sheer Extra™ - cut-away, permanent
• Sulky Cut-Away Plus™ - cut-away, permanent
• Sulky Solvy™ - water soluble
• Sulky Tender Touch™ - cut-away, permanent
• Sulky KK 2000™ Temporary Spray Adhesive

Design & Procedure:
This was a remake of a purchased turtleneck sweater. We carefully cut off the collar and marked where we wanted the scoop neck to be, then we zig-zagged around the cut edge.

• Open the side seams of the sweater so it will lay flat.
• Cut a piece of Sulky Soft 'n Sheer Extra that is larger than the embroidery design.
• Fuse it to the wrong side of the sweater where the design will be stitched.
• Hoop a piece of Sulky Cut-Away Plus.
• Lightly spray the Cut-Away Plus with Sulky KK 2000 and smooth the Soft 'n Sheer side of the sweater over it. *The KK 2000 will hold the garment in place, yet allow you to reposition as needed.*
• Spray KK 2000 onto a piece of Solvy that is larger than the embroidery and smooth it over the area to be embroidered. *The Solvy will keep the stitches from "sinking" into the knit.*
• Slide the hoop onto the machine. Check the position/ placement of the design with templates or the design positioning feature on the machine.
• Once the garment is positioned, use the "baste in the hoop" option to baste the garment to the hooped Cut-Away Plus and Solvy.
• Embroider your chosen design.
• Remove the basting and gently pull away the excess Solvy; use a damp cloth or Q-Tip to remove any remaining bits. Use a blunt-end scissors to carefully cut away the excess Cut-Away Plus from around the outside of the design as a whole.
• Fuse a layer of Tender Touch over the back of the embroidery to prevent irritation to the skin from the stitching.
• Reconstruct the sweater, applying the trim to the neck line and sewing the side seams.

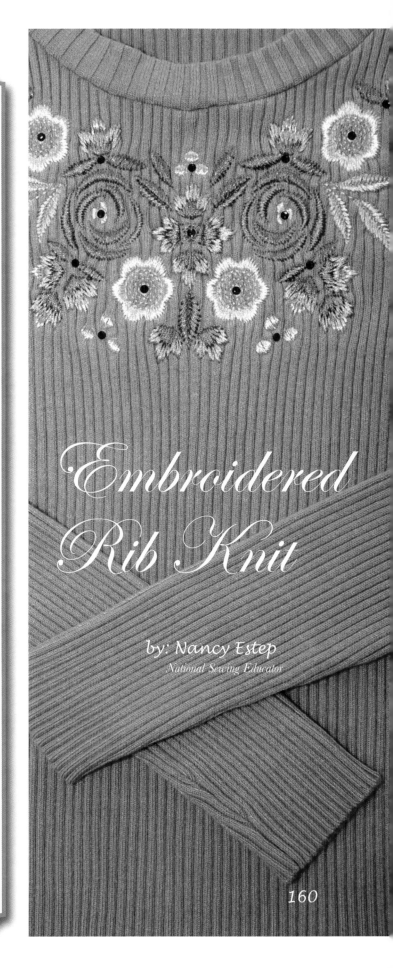

Embroidered Rib Knit

by: Nancy Estep
National Sewing Educator

160

Satin/Sateen

by Evelyn Byler
Designer for Sulky

Recipe for Success

Characteristics:

A lustrous silk in which the filling is so arranged as to bind the warp
as seldom as possible, and spaced so that practically nothing shows but the warp.

Needles:
- Schmetz Embroidery, Size 14/90

Stabilizer:
- Sulky Heat-Away Clear Film™ - heats away

Thread:
- Sulky Top Quality 40 wt. Rayon - top
- Sulky 60 wt. Polyester Bobbin Thread

- Sulky KK 2000™ Temporary Spray Adhesive

Design & Procedure:
The design is from Joyce Drexler's Cactus Punch Embroidery Card #107, Design #10703 Hummingbird.
The fabric is Robert Kaufman's Radiance. The Pillow project is from Sulky book #900B-17,
An Updated Supplement to Sulky's Secrets to Successful Stabilizing.

- Hoop a piece of Sulky Heat-Away with the bumpy side up.
- Spray Sulky KK 2000 evenly on the surface of the Heat-Away.
- Place the hoop on a flat surface and carefully drape the center of the fabric over the center of the hoop.
- Use your fingers to gently smooth and press the fabric down onto the Heat-Away. Check placement.
- Attach the hoop to the embroidery unit. Adjust as needed to position the needle correctly.
- Embroider, following the recommended Sulky 40 wt. Rayon Thread color changes.

- Remove the hoop from the machine. Carefully lift the fabric along the design margins and gently remove the fabric from the Heat-Away.
- Remove any remaining Heat-Away with a dry iron set to the correct temperature for the fabric used. The fabric may pucker as the stabilizer melts, but it will relax again once the removal is completed.
- When little waxy balls form, brush them off or use a lint roller to remove them.
- For detailed information on constructing the pillow, see the project in Sulky Book #900B-17.

Screening

Embroider on Screening

by: Peggy Dilbone
National Sewing Educator

162

Recipe for Success

Characteristics:
*A fun, colorful screening fabric with an uneven surface.
Phifer "Pet Screen" is a strong, vinyl-coated polyester.*

Needles:
• Schmetz Embroidery, Size 11/75

Thread:
• Sulky 40 wt. Rayon

Stabilizers:
• Two layers of Sulky Tear-Easy™ - tear-away
• Sulky Solvy™ - water soluble
• Sulky KK 2000 Temporary Spray Adhesive

Design & Procedure:
*Peggy made this tote as a serger project using an embroidery design
from the "Sew Many Designs" design pack - Monkeys & More.*

• Print a template of the embroidery design from your
  software.
• Hoop two layers of Sulky Tear-Easy tautly (layered in
  opposite directions).
• Slide the hoop onto the embroidery arm and baste the
  outline of the embroidery on the stabilizer only.
• Remove the embroidery hoop from the machine.
• Center the printed template on the screening, with the
  center of the designs approximately 4-1/2" from the top
  edge of the screening.
• Spray Sulky KK 2000 onto the Tear-Easy in the hoop,
  and slide the hoop back onto the embroidery arm.
• Center the embroidery template over the basted area of
  the stabilizer. Pin the screening to the stabilizer at each
  corner to hold it in place, then remove the template.
• Lay down the appliqué fabric and trim, then spray a
  piece of Sulky Solvy with KK 2000 and place it, tacky
  side down, on top of the fabric before doing the satin
  stitching.
  *The Solvy layer will allow the stitches to ride on top
  of the fabric and not sink into it for a much better look.*
• Embroider your chosen design.
• Remove the basting threads. Carefully tear away the
  Tear-Easy, one layer at a time. Pull away the excess
  Solvy and use a damp cloth to remove any that remains.

*Screening fabric and directions for the bag are on the
DVD "Sassy Serger Screen Bag" by Peggy Dilbone.
The DVD and Screening Fabric are available at
www.PeggyDdesigns.com.
This project, except for the embroidery,
was completely done on a serger
with cover stitch and chain stitch.*

Make Beautiful Edges

by: Nancy Estep
National Sewing Educator

Silk Tweed

Recipe for Success

Characteristics:
A coarse, rugged, often nubby silk fabric made in various twill weaves and used chiefly for suits and coats.

Needles:
- Schmetz Embroidery, Size 12/80

Thread:
- The Sulky 40 wt. Rayon color was chosen to be a tone-on-tone interpretation, bringing out one of the colors of the fabric. A very suble effect, but classic.

Stabilizers:
- 2 layers of Sulky Tear-Easy™ - tear-away, temporary
- Sulky Solvy™ - water soluble
- Sulky KK 2000™ Temporary Spray Adhesive

Design & Procedure:
Nancy made this suit and embroidered the fabric first, then cut out the sleeve and back of the skirt, so that she had more control of placement. She then made adjustments to the pattern before construction. Embroidery is from the Husqvarna Viking Design Collection by Anna Haraldson - "Edging Excellence".

- Hoop two layers of Sulky Tear-Easy tautly (layered in opposite directions) and lightly spray the top layer with Sulky KK 2000. Position the fabric on top of the stabilizer.
- Slide the hoop onto the machine. Check the position/placement of the design with templates or the design positioning feature on the machine. *The KK 2000 will hold the fabric in place, yet allow you to reposition as needed.*
- Once the fabric is positioned, place a layer of Sulky Solvy on top, then use the "baste in the hoop" option to baste the fabric to the hooped Tear-Easy, and the Solvy in place on top. *The Solvy layer will allow the stitches to ride on top of the fabric and not sink into it for a much better look.*
- Embroider your chosen design.
- Remove the basting and remove the excess Solvy. Carefully tear away the Tear-Easy, one layer at a time.
- Once the embroidery is done, lightly spray the pattern pieces with KK 2000 and smooth them onto the embroidered fabric. Cut out the pattern pieces.
- Construct the garment per pattern instructions.

Suede Leather

Recipe for Success

Characteristics:
A firm, dense fabric made from hides that have been processed. This suede had some give to it. Note: Never iron on the right side of leather as it will leave a mark.

Needles:
• Schmetz Stretch, Size 14/90

Thread:
• Sulky 40 wt. Rayon in the needle and Sulky Bobbin Thread in the bobbin. *Sue matched the colors in the blouse when she chose the thread for the design.*

Stabilizers:
• Two layers of Sulky Tear-Easy™ - tear-away, or one layer of Sulky Sticky+™ - self-stick, tear-away
• Sulky Solvy™ - water soluble (only on Suede Leather not on authentic Leather)
• Sulky KK 2000™ Temporary Spray Adhesive

Procedure:
This was a purchased suede leather jacket.

• Hoop two layers of Sulky Tear-Easy tautly (layered in opposite directions) and lightly spray the top layer with Sulky KK 2000 before putting the hoop on the machine. *Or, secure Sticky+ in the hoop, score the release sheet and remove it from the inside of the hoop.*
• Slide the hoop onto the machine, then place the garment on top of the hoop. Check the position/placement of the design with templates or the design positioning feature on the machine. *The KK 2000 will hold the garment in place, yet allow you to reposition as needed.*
• Once the garment is positioned, place a layer of Sulky Solvy on top. DO NOT BASTE as it will make holes in the Suede. *The Solvy layer will allow the stitches to ride on top of the fabric and not sink into it for a much better finished look.*
• Embroider your chosen design.
• Carefully tear away the Tear-Easy (or Sticky+), one layer at a time. If you used Solvy (only on Suede Leather), use a damp towel to remove any Solvy that remains.

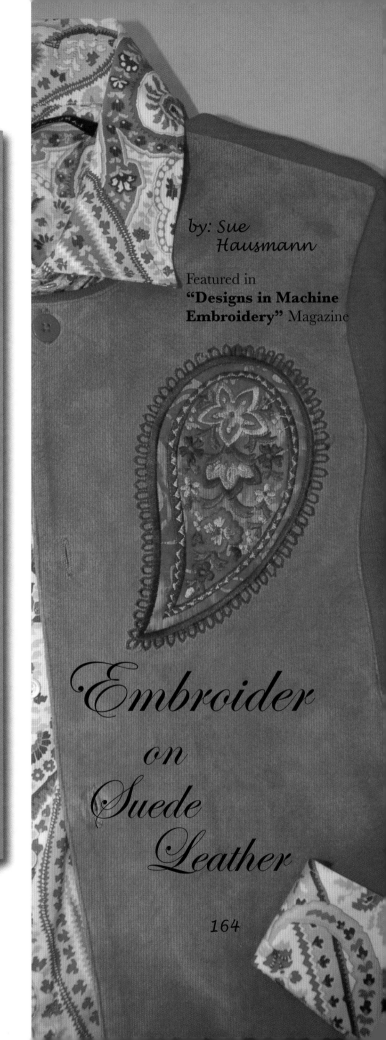

by: Sue Hausmann

Featured in **"Designs in Machine Embroidery"** Magazine

Embroider on Suede Leather

164

Sweater Knit

by: Sue Hausmann

Sweater Knit

Recipe for Success

Characteristics:
A small-ribbed, lightweight knitted fabric that has a reasonable amount of stretch to it.

Needles:
- Schmetz Embroidery, Size 12/80

Thread:
- Sulky 40 wt. Rayon - 388 colors to choose from

Stabilizers:
- SulkyTender Touch™ - iron-on, permanent
- Sulky Solvy™ - water soluble
- 2 layers of Tear-Easy™ - tear-away, temporary

Design & Procedure:
This was a purchased sweater with embroidery from the Husqvarna Viking Design Collection by Terry Fox.

- Give the Sulky Tender Touch a "blast" of steam before fusing to pre-shrink it.
- With the maximum stretch of the Tender Touch lengthwise on the garment, fuse it to the wrong side of the sweater in the area to be embroidered. Don't worry about the size of the Tender Touch being larger than the embroidery design, and do not "over fuse" as you will pull the excess Tender Touch away from the garment after embroidering.
- Hoop two layers of Sulky Tear-Easy tautly (layered in opposite directions) and lightly spray the top layer with Sulky KK 2000 before putting the hoop on the embroidery machine.
- Slide the hoop onto the machine, then smooth the garment on top of the Tear-Easy. Check the position/placement of the design with templates or the design positioning feature on the machine. The KK 2000 will hold the garment in place, yet allow you to reposition as needed.
- Once the garment is positioned, place a layer of Sulky Solvy on top, then use the "baste in the hoop" option to baste the garment to the hooped Tear-Easy and the Solvy on top. The Solvy will allow the stitches to ride on top of the fabric and not sink into it for a much better look.
- Embroider your chosen design.
- Remove the basting and the excess Solvy. Carefully tear away the excess Tear-Easy, one layer at a time. Pull the excess Tender Touch away from the wrong side of the sweater around the outside of the design and trim it away with a blunt-tip, bent scissors.

by: Eileen Roche

Editor of . . .
Designs in Machine
Embroidery Magazine
and Tamara Evans

Sweatshirt Knit

Recipe for Success

Characteristics:
A heavy, closely-knit fabric that does stretch.

Needles:
• Schmetz Ballpoint Embroidery, Size 14/90

Thread:
• Beautiful Sulky 40 wt. Rayon

Stabilizer:
• Sulky Soft 'n Sheer™ - permanent, cut-away
• Sulky Solvy™ - water soluble
• Sulky Tender Touch™ - permanent, iron-on

Design & Procedure:

A purchased sweatshirt that was disassembled, embroidered and reconstructed into an asymmetrical jacket (find complete directions on the CD in the back of this book). Embroidery designs are for the Magna-Hoop, from Designs in Machine Embroidery's "Embroider It Yourself - Scrumptious Sweats" CD.

• Fuse Sulky Tender Touch to the wrong side of the entire front placket.
• Use printed templates to create the embroidery layout. To create the continuous vine, position the three templates on the placket strip. Make sure the embroidery designs actually touch. Place the last template at the bottom. Apply target stickers (aligning the crosshairs of the template with the target sticker) and remove all templates.
• Hoop Sulky Soft 'n Sheer. Insert the metal frame of the Magna-Hoop into the hoop. Place the placket on the hoop, keeping the placket edge parallel to the hoop.
• Position the medium rectangular acrylic frame on top. If necessary, move the placket so it's centered in the opening.
• Snap the magnets in place and attach the hoop to the machine. Center the needle over the first target sticker. Trace the design to make sure it fits in the opening.
• Remove the target sticker and cover with Sulky Solvy, *which will keep the stitches from sinking into the knit.* Baste, then embroider the design.
• Remove the placket from the hoop. Reposition the placket, adding more stabilizer if necessary. Hoop, align and embroider the remaining designs. Follow the same steps to embroider the bodice.
• Once completed, remove excess stabilizer.

It's Just a Towel

by: Eileen Roche
Editor of "Designs in Machine Embroidery Magazine"

Toweling

Recipe for Success

Characteristics:
A woven or knitted fabric with loops that can peek through embroidery if not stitched with a topper like Sulky Solvy.

Needles:
- Schmetz Embroidery, Size 14/90

Thread:
- Sulky 40 wt. Poly Deco Thread - *can be laundered with brightners or bleach.*

Stabilizers:
- Sulky Solvy™ - *water soluble*
- Sulky Tear-Easy™ - *tear-away, temporary*
- Sulky KK 2000™ Temporary Spray Adhesive

Design & Procedure:
A purchased towel transformed into a Monogrammed Tote using designs from the book, "Machine Embroidered Monograms for the Home" by Marie Zinno and Eileen Roche.

- Hoop Sulky Tear-Easy stabilizer in a large hoop. Insert the metal frame of the Jumbo Magna-Hoop.
- Place the towel over the frame, centering the template/target sticker in the hoop. Place the frame over the towel and snap the magnets into place.
- Attach the hoop to the machine and position the needle over the template/target sticker. Remove the template/target sticker and place a piece of Solvy over the design area. Use the magnets to hold the Solvy in place, or spray it with Sulky KK 2000 Temporary Spray Adhesive and finger-press it in place. Baste.
- Embroider the monogram.
- Carefully remove the excess stabilizer.
- Fold the towel just above the monogram (this will be the top of the bag) and pin the folded flap onto the towel at the sides. Baste to hold the flap at the edges.
- Lay the towel on a flat surface, right side up, and bring the lower edge of the towel to the top of the border. Pin at the sides and sew them together with a ½" seam allowance on each side.
- Box the bottom of the bag by folding the pointed corner at the bag bottom to form a right triangle, centering the sewn seam. Sew across the triangle, 2 ½" from the point. Repeat for the opposite corner.
- Add two straps at the top of the bag, stitching through the bag flap. Reinforce the stitching at the end of the straps.

T-Shirt Knit

Recipe for Success

Characteristics:
*A lightweight, knitted fabric that
has a reasonable amount of stretch to it.*

Needles:
• Schmetz Embroidery or Ballpoint, Size 12/80

Thread:
• Sulky 40 wt. Rayon and Sulky Bobbin Thread

Stabilizers:
• Sulky Heat-Away™ - iron-away, temporary
• Sulky Soft 'n Sheer Extra™ - iron-on, permanent
• Sulky Tender Touch™ - iron-on, permanent
• Sulky KK 2000™ Temporary Spray Adhesive

Design & Procedure:
*These were purchased T-shirts that were embroidered
with a design from Joyce Drexler's Pressed Leaves 1
by Great Embroidery Designs. www.sulky.com*

• Cut a piece of Sulky Soft 'n Sheer Extra that is large
enough to fit entirely in the hoop, and iron it onto the
wrong side of the shirt where the embroidery will be
stitched.
• Hoop your garment.
• Lightly spray Sulky KK 2000 onto the bumpy side of
a piece of Heat-Away and smooth it onto the right side
of the T-shirt.
• Attach the hoop to the machine. Check the position/
placement of the design with templates or the design
positioning feature on the machine.
• Use the "baste in the hoop" option to baste everything
together. The Heat-Away keeps the stitches from
becoming embedded into the knit and gives a crisper,
sharper looking design.
• Embroider the design of your choice.
• Remove the basting and tear away the excess Heat-
Away. Remove any remaining Heat-Away with a dry
iron set to the correct temperature for the fabric used.
When little waxy balls form, brush them off or use a
lint roller to remove them.
• To prevent the stitches from
irritating sensitive skin, iron
a pinked piece of Tender
Touch over the wrong side
of the finished embroidery.

by Patti Lee
*Editor, Designer and
Sulky Vice-President
Consumer Relations*

168

Create a "No Stress" Appliqué

"Fashionette"
by Loralie Harris

Tulle

Recipe for Success

Characteristics:
A fine, often-starched net of silk, rayon, or nylon, used especially for veils and tutus.

Needle & Foot:
- Schmetz Topstitch or Embroidery, Size 14/90 when using Sulky Original Metallic Threads
- Spring-loaded, Free-Motion Foot

Threads:
- Use Sulky Metallic #7020 multi-color on the top and in the bobbin, or use Sulky Clear Polyester Thread in the bobbin. Wind the bobbin half-full at a slow speed.

Stabilizers:
- Sulky Fabri-Solvy™ - water soluble
- Sulky Tear-Easy™ - optional
- Sulky Soft 'n Sheer™ - optional
- Sulky KK 2000™ Temporary Spray Adhesive

Design & Procedure:
Loralie's Fashionette™ Peach Sequin Shiner™ Appliqué from her fanciful fabric collection "Mermania" is stitched using a free-motion, straight-stitch technique.

- Print out the pattern from the CD at the back of this book and use a water soluble marker to trace the line drawing and numbers onto Sulky Fabri-Solvy.
- Lay a piece of crinoline over a piece of Sulky Fabri-Solvy (the design will show through for fabric placement).
- Rough cut the paper pattern pieces, leaving about a 1/4" margin. Lightly spray them with Sulky KK 2000 and smooth them onto your appliqué fabric choices.
- Cut out the fabric pieces on the drawn line. As you place each fabric piece over the Fabri-Solvy and crinoline, remove the paper and place a small dab of fabric glue on the back of the fabric pieces and lay the fabrics, matching the numbers.
- Overlay the entire glued design with a piece of tulle. Pin.
- Starting in the center of the design, free-motion straight stitch, outlining around all the fabrics and design lines.
- Trim away the excess Fabri-Solvy and net, leaving a 1/8" margin all around.
- Soak in warm water. Roll in a towel and let dry. Iron using a press cloth.
- Back the appliqué area of the garment with either Tear-Easy or Soft 'n Sheer, lightly sprayed with KK 2000. Place the appliqué in your desired location and stitch over all the previously stitched lines.
- Carefully remove the excess stabilizer.

See other Free-Motion Fashionette Designs and Fabric Kits available from www.loraliedesigns.com

Scroll Work

by: Sue Hausmann

Tweed

Recipe for Success

Characteristics:
A coarse, rugged, often nubby woolen fabric made in various twill weaves and used chiefly for suits and coats.

Needles:
- Schmetz Embroidery, Size 14/90 when using Sulky 40 wt. Rayon Threads

Thread:
- The Sulky 40 wt. Rayon color was chosen to be a tone-on-tone interpretation, bringing out one of the colors of the fabric. A very subtle effect, but classic.

Stabilizers:
- 2 layers of Sulky Tear-Easy™ - tear-away, temporary
- Sulky Solvy™ - water soluble
- Sulky KK 2000™ Temporary Spray Adhesive

Design & Procedure:
This was a purchased, purple/black/white/gray tweed jacket on which we added purple (outlined in black) embroidery from the Husqvarna Viking Design Collection #117 Mega Borders.

- Use a seam ripper to open the front lining to the facing seam; fold and tape the lining out of the way so that you can embroider through the jacket fabric only.
- Hoop two layers of Sulky Tear-Easy tautly (layered in opposite directions), and lightly spray the top layer with Sulky KK 2000 Temporary Spray Adhesive before putting the hoop on the embroidery machine.
- Slide the hoop onto the machine, then place the garment on top of the hoop. Check the position/placement of the design with templates or the design positioning feature on the machine. The KK 2000 will hold the garment in place, yet allow you to reposition as needed.
- Once the garment is positioned, place a layer of Sulky Solvy on top, which will allow the stitches to ride on top of the fabric and not sink into it for a much better look. Use the "baste in the hoop" option to baste the garment to the hooped Tear-Easy, and the Solvy to the garment.
- Embroider your chosen design.
- Remove the basting and remove the excess Solvy.
- Carefully tear away the Tear-Easy, one layer at a time.

by:
Dorothy Martin
National Educator and Designer

Velvet

Recipe for Success

Characteristics:
Velvet is a textile that is woven on a special loom. It is a tufted fabric in which the cut threads are very evenly distributed, giving it its distinct feel.

Needles:
• Schmetz Metallic, Size 12/80

Thread:
• Top Quality Sulky Metallics on top
• Sulky Polyester Invisible Thread in the bobbin

Stabilizers:
• Sulky Tear-Easy™ - tear-away, temporary
• Sulky Solvy™ - water soluble
• Sulky KK 2000™ Temporary Spray Adhesive

Designs & Procedure:
The velvet is from JB Martin. Designs from www.criswellembroidery.com and Inspira

• Since velvet is fragile, it is wise to avoid dense designs because the constant needle penetrations can damage it.
• The nap on cotton and cotton blend velvets are more forgiving than on 100% rayon. The nap will appear richer if the nap direction is toward the top or head of the project.
• When embroidering on velvet, reduce the top tension and speed. Avoid black outlining.
• Hoop one layer of Tear-Easy, then spray it with Sulky KK 2000; finger-press the velvet on top and spray it with KK 2000. Smooth two layers of Sulky Solvy on top to keep the pile upright.
• Attach the hoop to the machine. Slide one layer of Tear-Easy under the hoop. Check the position/placement of the design with templates or the design positioning feature on the machine.
• Use the baste-in-the-hoop option to baste everything together.
• Embroider your chosen design.
• When embroidering with Sulky Sliver or Holoshimmer, keep the spool vertical on the spool pin.
• Trim threads as you go, rather than later when other colors are stitched on top.
• To remove the stabilizers, tear them away one at a time like you would tear a check from a checkbook.

Vinyl

Recipe for Success

Characteristics:
A tough, slippery, synthetic, flexible, shiny plastic fabric derived from ethylene.

Needles:
- Schmetz Embroidery, Size 14/90

Thread:
- Top Quality Sulky 40 wt. Rayon

Stabilizers:
- Sulky Tender Touch™ - iron-on, permanent
- 2 layers of Tear-Easy™ - tear-away, temporary
- Sulky KK 2000™ Temporary Spray Adhesive

Design & Procedure:
This was a purchased raincoat with a flannel lining that was embroidered with rainboots from www.emblibrary.com

- Spray Sulky KK 2000 onto one layer of Sulky Tear-Easy, then smooth a second layer (in the opposite direction) on top of it; secure them in your machine embroidery hoop.
- Slide the hoop onto the embroidery arm and baste the outline of the embroidery on the stabilizer only.
- Remove the hoop from the machine.
- Spray KK 2000 onto the hooped Tear-Easy and slide the hoop back onto the embroidery arm.
- Finger-press the vinyl raincoat into position.
- Embroider your chosen design.
- Remove the jump-stitches from the front, and the loose bobbin threads from the back. Carefully tear away the Tear-Easy.
- Use pinking shears to cut a piece of Tender Touch slightly larger than the embroidery, and quickly iron it on the back, over the embroidery stitches, to keep them from irritating the child's skin.

Embroidered on a professional embroidery machine by:

Alyson Prater
Action Embroidery
Cartersville, GA 30120
770-387-9066

Made for her daughter, Isabelle, pictured with their dog, Deuce.

Monogrammed Pillowcases

*If you love this beautiful Monogram Design, then you will want to join the **Sulky Embroidery Design Club** to get the whole alphabet. This is just a preview of what is offered only to our world-wide membership. Join anytime and receive a whole year's worth of exclusive artwork by best-selling embroidery artists, Carol Ingram and Joyce Drexler.*

by Carol Ingram

Featuring Sulky Tear-Easy, Fabri-Solvy and
Sticky+ Stabilizers.

*"This Pillowcase can be a serger project
or simply sewn on the machine. An
optional ruffle may be inserted where
the piping is at the base of the header
band on the pillow case.*

*An option for children is to embroider
kid's monograms on a plain header
band, while using kid's prints for the pillowcase. With all the decorator fabrics
available, there are many choices for
gift pillowcases including wedding,
birthday and anniversary gifts."*
--- Carol

Materials:

Queen-Size Pillowcases:
- 3/4 yd. satin or high-count cotton
- 1/4 yd. fabric for header band -
  cut one 14" x 44" piece
- 1-1/2" x 45" coordinating fabric
  strip for piping along the header band
- 1-1/4 yd. cotton cording (size 80)

Header Band
and Embroidery:
- Sulky Tender Touch™ Stabilizer
- Sulky Tear-Easy™ Stabilizer
- Sulky Solvy™ Stabilizer
- Sulky KK 2000™ Temporary Spray
  Adhesive
- Sulky 40 wt. Rayon Threads
  to coordinate with the fabric

- Measure Pillow for cutting size needed
- Monogram Letter size 3" (Carol used
  her designs from the *"Sulky Embroidery
  Design Club Collection" www.sulky.com*
- Cording/Piping or Zipper Foot
- 14" Quilter's Ruler, Mat and
  Rotary Cutter
- General Sewing Supplies

Preparation for Embroidery:

1. Iron Sulky Tender Touch onto the wrong side of the Header Band.

Fold the Header Band in half, matching the short ends. Press the fold. Fold in half again, matching the long sides. Press the fold.

2. Unfold. Turn up the long side so that the cut edge matches the center fold line. Press the fold.

3. Unfold. Set aside.

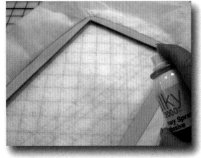

4. Place two layers of Sulky Tear-Easy in the hoop. Lightly spray the top layer with Sulky KK 2000.

174

Embroider:

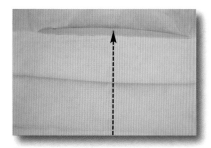 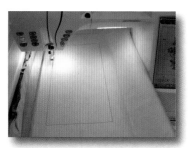 

5. Smooth the header band over the tacky Tear-Easy, lining up the center folds with the center marks on the hoop.

Spray the fabric with KK 2000 and smooth a piece of Sulky Solvy over it.

6. You can embroider the entire design in a mega hoop or you can do three hoopings in a smaller hoop.

Select "baste" or "fix".

7. In the software editing program, Carol chose the intial "D" and added a floral flourish to both sides. She also added more of the same flowers around the "D".

Embroider. Clip the threads. Remove the Solvy, then tear away the Tear-Easy, one layer at a time.

Construction:

1. Cut the Cotton/Satin for the body of the pillowcase, 24" x 38-1/2".

2. Make piping from the cotton cording by wrapping the 1-1/2" x 44" piece of fabric over the cording (wrong sides together) and stitching close to the cording, using a cording foot. Lay the piping strip along the 38-1/2" edge of the pillow-case and stitch it in place.

3. With right sides together, lay the 38-1/2" piped edge of the pillow-case onto the embroidered header and stitch close to the piping. Press.

4. Fold the pillowcase in half lengthwise, with the header band opened out, and stitch the side and bottom seams. Press.

Fold the header back in place and pin; then stitch to secure.

Oh, the sheer pleasure of sleeping on satin sheets and pillowcases.
Now you can make someone's dreams come true by embroidering
one of Carol's "Designer Alphabet Letters with Flourishes"
which makes the perfect, personalized gift!

Embroidered and / or Appliquéd Overshirts

"What fun you will have creating your own theme overshirts. During Fall and Winter I tend to live in my embellished overshirts. They cheer me up during the gloomy winter months and they get me loads of compliments when I wear them to our local quilt shops or to 'Pickin-on-the-Square' on Saturday nights. And they are just right for wearing in our convertible in the Spring and Summer here in the mountains of NC." --- Joyce

Joyce Drexler, on the left, with Sue Hausmann taping the **PBS-TV Show,**
"AMERICA SEWS WITH SUE HAUSMANN". Sue's appliqués were cut from a
Thimbleberries™ flannel print and Joyce's from a Benartex™ fabric.

"Black-eyed Susans" by Joyce Drexler

Featuring Sulky® Soft 'n Sheer™
and Totally Stable™ Stabilizers

So many readers have asked for the directions for embellishing the shirt I wore on the cover of my book, "Weekend Quilting with Sulky" that we have included them here for you.

Materials

- Computerized Sewing Machine with Embroidery Unit and Hoops - 14/90 Topstitch Needle
- Edge Foot, Free-Motion Foot and a Clear, Open-toe Appliqué Foot
- Embroidery Design Cards - all by Joyce Drexler - www.sulky.com:
  - For the "Christmas Cats" - Cactus Punch Sig. Series #82 "Winter"
  - For the "Grand Fleur" - Great Embroidery Designs - "Grand Flowers Collection" #CMD-JD2 Designs #22827 and #22834
  - For the "Fern Shirt" - Great Embroidery Designs - "Jumbo Fabulous Ferns" #111880
- Denim shirt with 1 or 2 pockets and regular buttons - not snaps
- 2/3 yd. coordinating fabric cut as follows: *(Note: Extra fabric has been allowed in case you need to cut some strips on the bias if your shirt has curved pockets.)*
  - Cut one each: 1" x 15" strip; 1" x 24" strip; 1-1/4" x 25" strip; 2" x 17" strip; 2" x 20" strip
  - Cut three: 1-1/2" x width of fabric
- 30 wt. Blendables® Cotton Thread #4057 Fresh Butter for Grand Fleur Shirt
- All-purpose sewing thread that matches the topstitching thread on the shirt
- Various Sulky 40 wt. Rayon Threads for embroidery
- Sulky Cotton Blendables® Threads or Sulky 30 wt. Rayon Thread used for the blanket stitching
- Sulky Black Soft 'n Sheer, Black Totally Stable, Black Tear-Easy, and Sticky+
- Steam-A-Seam Lite™ Fusible Web • General Sewing Supplies
- Rotary Cutter and Mat • Bias-Tape Maker in several widths (optional)

Prepare the Overshirt for Embroidery:

1. Remove and set aside the placket buttons and pockets.

Lay the shirt, front side up, on a cutting mat. To remove the tails, lay your ruler in a straight line across the bottom of the shirt, just above the end of the side seam hems. Cut.

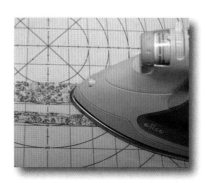

2. Once the pockets are removed there can be a color difference between where the pocket(s) were and the rest of the shirt. To turn this into a positive, we will create a fabric frame for the embroidery by covering the seam lines with strips of coordinating fabric.

If your shirt only has one pocket and you would like a second pocket on the other side, use the removed pocket to mark where a second pocket could be and cut it out of a coordinating fabric (like Christmas Cats).

3. Cut a piece of Black Totally Stable at least 1" bigger than the pocket size and use a dry iron to press it onto the inside of the shirt front, covering the pocket area completely.

4. Cut a 1" x 15" strip of coordinating floral fabric on the straight of grain. Turn under and press the long edges to a finished width of 1/2" (1/4" on each long side so they butt together in the middle). Or, you can use a 1/2" bias-tape maker.

5. Cut the 1/2" x 15" strip in half to make two 1/2" x 7-1/2" strips. Place one covering the bottom seam line of the missing pocket; pin in place. Place the other one as the top frame piece so that the bottom one extends slightly more towards the placket to add a bit more interest. Be sure that the frame is square with the shirt front; adjust as needed.

Set up the Machine:
- Thead the top and bobbin with Sulky 30 wt. Cotton Blendables® (We used #4057 Fresh Butter.)
- Size 14/90 Topstitch Needle
- Select the Blanket Appliqué Stitch
- Attach an All-Purpose Foot

6. Turn under 1/4" on the short ends of the top and bottom fabric frame pieces; appliqué them on with a blanket stitch on both sides and both ends.

7. Cut a 2" x 17" piece of the same floral fabric, turn under 1/2" on each long side (as in #4 or use a 1" bias-tape maker) and press. Cut the strip in half to make two 1" x 8-1/2" strips. Place them vertically over the side seam lines of the missing pocket to frame the area. Pin in place, then blanket stitch (as in #6 above).

Determine Embroidery Placement:

1. Mark the center needle position in the fabric frame. Because the pocket on our shirt was a large one, we enlarged the embroidery design size in the machine so that the top of the flower overlapped the fabric framing. Printing out a copy of the embroidery design, as we did, can help you to decide where to place your flower.

TIP: *When the thread color used in the embroidery is a dark color or black, change your bobbin thread to black because sometimes the machine's tension will cause a tiny bit of the bobbin thread to show on the top, creating little white spots all over the embroidery. This is particularly important in finely stitched areas like the little trails being left by the ladybugs, or on the final outline stitch.*

2. Spray Sulky KK 2000 between two layers of Sulky Black Soft 'n Sheer. Spray KK 2000 on the top layer of the Soft 'n Sheer and place the shirt (with the still-attached Totally Stable side down) over it. Hoop them all together and slide the hoop onto your embroidery machine. Embroider the flower.

3. Unhoop and cut away the Soft 'n Sheer close to the stitching, then tear away the excess Totally Stable.

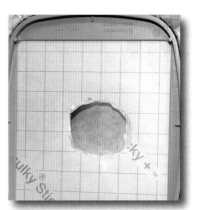

4. Hoop a piece of Sulky Sticky+ in your smallest available size hoop and set the pattern for just one ladybug.

Embroider ladybugs in a variety of places (see photo on page 177), like flying out of the removed pocket, below the pocket, on the other pocket, a shoulder, a few on the sleeve and above the cuff, as well as on the back.

Each time a ladybug is embroidered, pull the shirt from the Sticky+ and add a piece of Sticky+ (after removing the release sheet) that is larger than the hole, and stick it under the hole to patch it.

Repeat the procedure until all the ladybugs are embroidered where you want them. Rotate the ladybug's direction frequently.

5. Once the embroidery is completed in the area, tear away the excess Totally Stable and trim the Soft 'n Sheer close to the stitching as a whole.

Wrong side of shirt.

Binding the Shirt:

Extend strip 1/2" beyond collar band

1. Cut three 1-1/2" x width-of-fabric strips and sew them together lengthwise with 45° angle seams. Use a 3/4" bias tape maker or turn under a scant 3/8" on each long side (see #4 on p. 178). Starching the strip prior to ironing will help keep the folds pressed in and crisp.

Thread the machine with all-purpose sewing thread to match the color of the shirt's topstitching. Beginning on the right side as worn, open one fold of the pressed fabric and align that raw-edge end of the strip with the edge of the placket with 1/2" of the short end extending onto the collar band. Fold down the top extra 1/2" of the

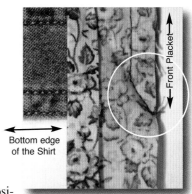

Front Placket

Bottom edge of the Shirt

floral fabric, even with the end of the button placket. Pin in place. Using the edge of the all-purpose foot as a guide along the fabric edge, set the needle position to a generous 1/4" from the edge of the shirt. Begin stitching with a backstitch at the joining point of the collar and button placket. Continue down the front of the shirt; stop stitching 1/4" from the bottom. With your needle down, turn the shirt and sew diagonally directly to the corner point at a 45° angle (see the photo on the right).

Placket edge

Bottom of shirt

Placket edge

Bottom of shirt

2. Take the shirt from the machine and trim all the threads. Turn the fabric strip against the angle stitching just done (wrong sides together), maintaining the pressed-under fold line.

   Finger-press the fabric strip following the angle you established with the corner stitching.

3. Fold the fabric strip back onto itself, aligning the raw edge with the bottom of the shirt. With the corner fold exactly at the corner of the shirt, pin in place.

4. Begin stitching at the edge, backstitch, and continue on to the next corner. Sew the second corner the same as the last, then up the front buttonhole placket.

5. Stop stitching a couple of inches from the edge of the collar band. Position the fabric so that it extends about 1/2" onto the collar band and trim away the excess. Fold down this remaining 1/2" (wrong sides together) and finish stitching up to the edge of the collar. Backstitch to secure.

> **Mitering Corners Tip:** *This method of mitering corners on trim is useful in many applications. It will work for mitering any angle corner. We will use the same method for the more sharply angled tips of the collar. Remember to stop at the spot where the seam allowances converge, then sew off at an angle, bisecting the corner. Fold the trim up on the stitching, and then back at an angle, aligning the edges. The corner fold needs to be exactly above the base corner.*

Inside corner

Inside neckband

6. Finish the binding around the outside edges of the shirt by folding the trim to the wrong side of the shirt. Maintain the pressed-in fold (which is the finished edge on the wrong side), and pin the trim in place all around the shirt. **It's important that the fold covers the line just stitched.**

   When a corner is reached, turn the trim to the wrong side of the shirt which now naturally forms the miter because of how you stitched the trim down at the corners the first time. Look at the front of the corner and note which side of the corner has the fullness. To minimize bulk, tuck in the corners on the wrong side of the shirt so the fullness goes in the opposite direction. When the miter on the wrong side is the way you want it, pin across the corner, catching both sides. Continue pinning until the entire shirt is pinned.

   Begin straight stitching in the ditch on the right side at the front collar band where the trim begins. Backstitch to secure the threads, and slowly and carefully stitch in the ditch around the entire shirt. Check all of the binding you have sewn down to see if any edges were not stitched; hand-stitch them down, if neccessary.

Cuff Trim Binding:

1. On the 1" x 24" fabric strip, fold each long edge in 1/4" and press, making a 1/2" finished piece. (You will not be making the final fold as you did on the shirt edge binding, since this will be applied to the top and not folded over the edge.)

2. Cut it into two 1/2" x 12" pieces. With the ends extending 1/4" beyond the edge, pin a strip along the top edge of each cuff. Thread the top and bobbin with #4057 Fresh Butter. Edge-stitch along the outside edges, turning under the short ends 1/4" as you get to them.

Since there was a flap on the original shirt pocket, there was an extra piece to bind.

Collar Trim Binding:

1. Make the collar trim by double-folding the 1-1/4" x 25" strip to a finished width of a **scant** 3/8". Apply this trim just as you applied the trim around the shirt. The strip is just slightly narrower to avoid covering the buttonholes in the collar tips.

Pocket Trim Binding:

1. Fold and press your 2" x 20" strip into binding and place the end of the strip at the top of the pocket; fold down 1/4" of the short end. Align the edge of the pocket and the folded short edge of the strip.

2. Begin stitching at the top a scant 1/4" from the edge; backstitch, and continue sewing to the corner. Then, sew slowly around the curve. Ease in the extra fabric in the curve. Continue to the other top corner, fold down 1/4", and stitch in place. Backstitch.

3. Clip the trim fabric in the corner curves. Turn the trim fabric to the wrong side of the pocket and pin in place. Pin the pocket over the original stitching lines. Using matching all-purpose sewing thread, stitch in the ditch at the edge of the trim to reattach the pocket. If there is a pencil divider in the pocket, restitch those lines as well.

4. Thread the top and bobbin with Sulky 30 wt. Blendables #4057 Fresh Butter and topstitch just along the outside edge of the trim to make certain the trim fabric is held securely in place. Sew the buttons back on the shirt. *Finished!*

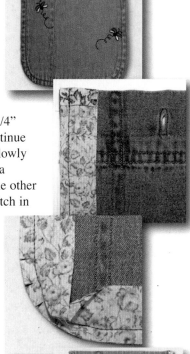

Create Full Fabric Cuffs as on the Cat and Fern Shirts:

1. If you are a woman using a man's shirt and you want to shorten the sleeve length, cut off the excess length allowing for a 4" faux cuff to be added.

2. Use the cut-off cuff as a template to draw a pattern. Use the pattern to cut 2 cuffs from the trim fabric for each sleeve (4 total).

3. To make one finished cuff, put the right sides of 2 cut pieces together and sew all the way around them, leaving the long straight edge open. Clip at rounded corners.

4. Turn the finished cuff right side out. Press. Turn a 1/2" fold to the wrong side along the open edge. Press.

5. Slip the finished cuff over the cut raw edge of the right side of the sleeve, matching raw edges. Pin in place.

6. Use an appliqué or blanket stitch, **width 2.5, length 4.0,** to sew down the folded-under edge of the trim to the sleeve.

7. Now you can add a button and buttonhole and the cuff can be turned back, if desired. Repeat steps 3 through 7 for the second cuff.

back

The shirt on the left was embroidered with ferns from Joyce Drexler's **"Jumbo Ferns"** embroidery card. The trim fabric is from McKenna Ryan's Fabric Collection (Sweet Pea Color 447) by Hoffman Fabrics. The shirt on the right was embroidered with a Mumm from Joyce's Grand Flower Collection 1 by Great Embroidery Designs. *www.sulky.com.*

Embroidering the "Christmas Cat "Shirts:

1. **For the Christmas Cats shirt,** we used the snowflakes on the Cactus Punch, Signature Series Card #82, WINTER. www.sulky.com.

2. A variety of Sulky Stabilizers could be used to back the areas being embroidered with snowflakes. Choose from Sulky Sticky+, Fabri-Solvy, or a liquid Solvy solution.

Cat on top of pocket

Appliquéing Prints:

1. Following the package directions, apply Steam-A-Seam2 Lite or regular Steam-A-Seam 2 to the print fabric.

2. **Cut out the fabric print designs next to the line (not on the line as it takes away some of the design).**

3. On the Cat Shirt, place them by the snowflakes and use a steam iron to fuse them to the shirt.

4. Thread the top and bobbin (wind the bobbin very slowly) with Sulky Clear or Smoke Polyester Invisible Thread.

5. Slip a piece of Sulky Tear-Easy under the appliqué to be stitched and stitch around the edges of the designs with a short length, straight stitch or open zig-zag. Gently tear away the Tear-Easy while supporting the stitching with your fingers.

184

Stabilizer Roll Holder

by Sue Hausmann
Sewing and Quilting "Edutainer"

and

Marie Duncan
Education Creative Coordinator
SVP Worldwide

"This great organizer will keep all of your rolls and packages of Sulky Stabilizers in order! Choose your favorite embroideries to decorate the pockets. We embroidered designs and design elements that were inspired by Sue 's Collection, "Happy Sewing" and then embroidered the name of each Sulky Stabilizer as well.

Now, it's fast and easy to find the Sulky Stabilizer that we need for any project!" - Sue and Marie

185

Cut the Fabrics:

1. Cut five 10" x 19-1/2" pieces of cream-colored denim for the pockets, and one 10" x 10" piece for the embroidery on the top.

2. Cut two 12" x 53" pieces of brown, tone-on-tone cotton for the base.

3. Cut three strips of 3" wide x the width of the brown, tone-on-tone cotton fabric for binding.

Embroider:

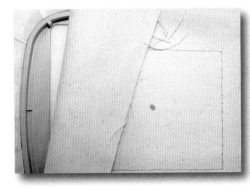

1. Tautly hoop 2 layers of Sulky Tear-Easy Stabilizer, layered in opposite directions.

(Sue and Marie used the 250 x 140 hoop on their machine.)

2. Slide the hoop onto the machine. With a wash-out marker, mark the embroidery starting point on the denim, 5" down and 5" in from a 10" side, centered as shown. Baste one of the 10" x 19-1/2" pieces of denim to the stabilizer.

Materials

- Sewing/Embroidery Machine with Hoops
- 4-Thread Serger
- Denim Needle, Size 14/90
- Sulky 40 wt. Rayon Embroidery Threads
- Sulky 30 wt. Cotton or Cotton Blendables
- Sulky Bobbin Thread
- Sewing Thread
- Sue Hausmann's Cactus Punch, "Happy Sewing" Collection
- Adjustable Bias Binding Foot, Edge Stitching Foot or Zipper Foot
- Even-Feed Foot with Quilting Guide
- 1-1/8 yards Cream Colored Denim
- 1-2/3 yards of Brown, Tone-on-Tone Cotton
- Warm and Natural Batting
- 7 yards of 7/8" wide Ribbon
- 3 yds. of 3/8" wide Ribbon
- Sulky KK 2000 Temporary Spray Adhesive
- Roll of Sulky Tear-Easy Stabilizer
- Wash-out Marker
- General Sewing Supplies

3. Embroider your chosen design using the Sulky 40 wt. Rayon Threads called for in the design. Marie used the built-in lettering fonts in the embroidery machine to add the name of the stabilizer below the embroidery design. Repeat for the other 4 pockets, using a different Sulky Stabilizer name for each.

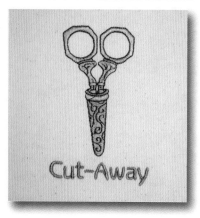

Change to the smallest appropriate hoop to embroider both a design and the word "Stabilizer" on the 10" x 10" piece for the top of your stabilizer holder.

Construct Your Base:

Set up the Machine for Quilting:

- Insert a size 14/90 Denim Needle
- Thread the top and bobbin with a matching color of Sulky 30 wt. Cotton Thread
- Select a straight stitch, length 2.5
- Attach an Even-Feed Foot and Quilting Guide

TIP: *Sue and Marie suggest using two pieces of batting to give nice body to the base so it will hang well and support the weight of the rolls of stabilizers. You could also use one layer of batting and one layer of Sulky Fuse 'n Stitch ironed onto the wrong side of the first 12" x 53" piece of brown, tone-on-tone fabric.*

---

1. Create a "Quilt Sandwich":

A. On a flat surface, lay one of the 12" x 53" pieces of brown, tone-on-tone fabric, wrong side up, and lightly spray it with Sulky KK-2000 Temporary Spray Adhesive.

B. Smooth a layer of Warm and Natural Batting over it. Then, lightly spray it with KK 2000.

C. Smooth the second layer of batting over it.

D. Lightly spray KK 2000 on the wrong side of the second 12" x 53" piece of brown, tone-on-tone fabric and smooth it over the batting.

2. Stitch vertical rows of straight stitching 1" apart all across the quilt sandwich, using your quilting guide to keep the lines evenly spaced. Just set it for 1" and keep it even with the edge of your fabric for the first row; thereafter use the previous line of stitching.

5. Thread the top and bobbin with a Sulky decorative thread to match the 3/8" ribbon color, select a straight stitch (length 2.5), and attach an edge-stitching foot or zipper foot. Place the 3/8" ribbon over the raw edge of the embroidered square.

Adjust the needle position so that you can top-stitch the ribbon close to the **inside** edge of the ribbon, through the embroidered square and backing. Begin stitching at a corner.

Miter the corners as you come to them and tuck the ribbon under on the last corner. Now, top-stitch on the **outer** edge of the ribbon, around all four sides.

3. Bind all four edges of your quilted sandwich, using your favorite binding technique.

4. Trim your 10" x 10" embroidered top piece to 6" x 6". Center it on your base so that the top of the embroidery is 1-3/4" down from the top. Pin.

Finish the Pockets:

1. Fold the 7/8" wide ribbon in half, wrong sides together, and finger-press. Starting at a corner, use either an edge-stitching foot, bias binding foot or a zipper foot to bind the **long edges** of each embroidered pocket with the 7/8" wide ribbon.

Wrap the ribbon around the edge of the canvas and stitch near the edge of the ribbon, catching both layers.

2. Fold each pocket in half lengthwise, wrong sides together, and use a 4-thread overlock stitch to serge the two unfinished edges together.

▲ serged top edge

Heat-Away

▼ folded bottom edge

Tear Away

3. Pin on the next pocket so that it overlaps 1" over the bottom one. Continue pinning and stitching over the 3/8" ribbon so that each pocket overlaps the previous one by about 1".

Attach the Pockets:

1. Starting at the bottom, pin the first pocket to the base, with the bottom of the bottom pocket being even with the top of the binding on the bottom of the base.

2. Lay the 3/8" ribbon over the top of the serged edge, turn the short ends under at the 2 corners, and topstitch in place close to both the inside and outside edges of the ribbon.

Iron-On

Hanging It:

1. Purchase an over-the-door hanger with three hooks. Sue and Marie made loops by cutting three 5" lengths of the 3/8" wide ribbon.

Fold under the raw ends or apply a fray-stopping liquid. Stitch them on the top of the organizer in positions to correspond with your hooks.

Beautiful Dogwoods

"My thread painting was inspired by my friend, Carol Rollick, who is a composite photographer. I will refer to the wallhanging as the canvas; the flowers, leaves and branches as elements; and the free-motion stitching as thread painting." - Chris

Experience the added dimension of bobbin-work.

Preparation:

1. Cut a 13" x 16" piece of black background fabric.

2. Cut an 11" x 14" piece of Sulky Fuse 'n Stitch. Following package directions, center and fuse this piece to the wrong side of the black fabric. This will be your "canvas".

3. **Print out the Dogwood Patterns found on the CD in the back of this book. The designs have already been reversed.**

4. Spray starch and press each of your "element fabrics" 3 times. To avoid white flaking, wait a few seconds each time before pressing to insure that the starch has soaked in well.

5. Cut the Steam-A-Seam2 Lite into four 10" x 10" pieces. Remove one of the release sheets from one of the Steam-A-Seam pieces, whichever one comes off the easiest. Smooth the remaining sheet, sticky side down, over the Dogwood pattern pieces and trace them using a Sharpie extra-fine, permanent-ink, black marker. Label each dogwood flower petal with the corresponding flower number. Repeat for the leaves and branches, noting the fabric colors on the branches.

6. Place the traced Steam-A-Seam patterns on the wrong side of the fabric that corresponds with the element color. Press lightly.

7. Rough-cut the element pieces, keeping them in properly numbered groups of 4 for the petals.

8. Remove the release paper from the fused element pattern pieces of the branches and use the placement guide to position them on your black background fabric.

by Chris Eichner

Featuring Sulky® Fuse 'n Stitch™ Stabilizer

Finished Size: 14" x 17"

Materials

- Sulky KK 2000™ Temporary Spray Adhesive
- Sulky Fuse 'n Stitch™ Permanent Stabilizer
- Sulky 40 wt. Rayon Thread:
  #1001 Bright White, #1023 Yellow, #1177
  Avocado, #1176 Med. Dk. Avocado, #1227
  Gold Green, #1170 Lt. Brown, #1508 Putty,
  #1005 Black, #1058 Tawny Brown,
  #1158 Dk. Maple
- Sulky Sliver™ Metallic Thread #8040
  Opalescent
- Sulky 30 wt. Cotton Blendables® #4001
  Parchment and #4009 Foliage
- Sulky Clear and Smoke Invisible Thread
- 1 yd. Steam-A-Seam2 Lite™
- 4 - 8-1/2" x 11" pieces of Fleece
- 3-ply Hand-painted Cotton floss:
  Watercolors by Caron – Tea Green
- Free-motion/Darning Foot
- Extra Bobbins
- Air Soluble Marking Pen
- Sharpie™ Extra-Fine, Black Marker
- Machine Needles:
  14/90 Embroidery and 14/90 Metallic
- Steam Iron and Pad
- Heavy Duty Spray Starch
- Optional: Extra Bobbin Case
- Optional: Couching, Open-toe or
  Applique Foot

Fabrics:
- 1-1/4 yd. black mottled or marbled cotton for
  background, border, backing and sleeve
- 1/8 yd. batik gold for border
- 1/8 yd. batik green for leaves and border

Element Fabrics:
- 1/8 yd. batik gray/green for branch
- 1/8 yd. batik rust for branches
- 1/8 yd. batik brown for branches
- 1/4 yd. off-white mottled or batik for petals
  and folded border

9. Repeat for the dogwood flowers, using
   the placement guide and matching petal
   numbers to arrange them on the
   background fabric, until all 7 flowers
   are placed.

10. Arrange leaves in the same manner.
    When you are satisfied with the
    placement, press with a steam iron to
    fuse everything in place.

Thread Painting the Canvas:

**Set up the Machine for
Free-motion Stitching:**
- Lower feed dogs or cover them
- Select straight stitch - length 0
- Lower upper thread tension slightly
- Insert a new 14/90 machine
  embroidery needle
- Attach a Free-Motion/Darning Foot
- Wind a bobbin **very slowly** with Sulky
  Polyester Smoke Invisible Thread

Branches:

To stitch the dark brown branches, thread the top with Sulky 40 wt. Rayon #1170, Light Brown.

1. Hold the top thread while you turn the hand wheel toward you to take one stitch. Pull up on the top thread to bring the Sulky Smoke Polyester Invisible Thread to the top of the project.

2. To tie on, hold the two thread tails in one hand, take a few small straight stitches, then cut the tails close to the fabric.

3. Select a narrow zig-zag stitch (about 3.0 width) and stitch a fairly close satin stitch the length of the branch. When the branch is complete, set the width to zero again and take a few straight stitches to tie off and lock the threads.

4. To move to the next dark brown branch, raise the presser foot to release the upper

tension, then easily move to the next branch. No need to cut the bobbin thread.

5. Change the top thread to #1058 Tawny Brown. Since the bobbin thread is still attached, it does not need to be brought up to the top. Just hold the top thread to prevent the thread from jamming, and begin stitching.

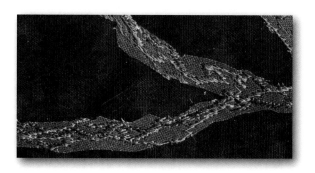

6. Stitch the lighter grey-tone branch the same way, only using #1170 Light Brown first, then highlighting with #1508 Putty.

193

Dogwood Flower Petals:

Select a straight stitch. Thread the top with Sulky 40 wt. Rayon #1001 Bright White and put Sulky Clear Invisible in the Bobbin. (Wind your bobbin very slowly and only about 1/2 full.)

1. Begin stitching following the outer edge of the petals; keep the contour of the

petals by working stitches towards the center. Raise the presser foot when moving the fabric to follow the contour of the other side of the petal to the center, leaving spaces for the fabric to show through.

3. Indentations of the Petal Tips:

With Sulky 40 wt. Rayon #1058 Tawny Brown on the top and Sulky Clear Invisible in the bottom, stitch the petal tips with a 1.5 or 2.0 width. Highlight using the Sulky 40 wt. Rayon #1158 Dk. Maple and add just a little Sulky 40 wt. Rayon #1023 Yellow toward the inside of each petal.

2. Shading:

Thread the machine with Sulky 30 wt. Blendables #4001 Parchment and continue in the same manner, shading mostly the center of the petals and some outside edges. Shade lightly with 30 wt. #4009 Foliage.

194

4. Change to a size 14/90 metallic needle. Further embellish the petals using Sulky Sliver™ Metallic #8040 Opalescent.

Place the spool on a vertical spool pin with a felt pad underneath. You will need to lower your top tension a bit more. Select straight stitch set at 0, choose several flowers and, sewing slowly, lightly stitch all of the petals of each chosen flower, just adding subtle glittery highlights as you follow the contour of the previous stitching.

Leaves:
Thread the top with Sulky 40 wt. Rayon #1176 Med. Dk. Avocado, and set your stitch width at 2.0 to 2.5.

1. Starting at the bottom, stitch the center vein of the leaf, then slightly ease back down this stitching line, flaring out every 1/4 inch or so to the right and left to create the vein lines. Stop just short of the edges of the leaves.

2. Change the top thread to Sulky 40 wt. Rayon #1177 Avocado and select a straight stitch set at 0. Do random straight stitching following the contour of the leaf. Don't get too carried away…you do want the fabric to continue to show through!

3. Change to Sulky 40 wt. Rayon #1227 Gold Green and use a small zig-zag stitch, width 2.5, to add some lighter highlights on some of the leaves.

4. Do the remaining green leaves in the same manner.

195

Bobbin-Work:
Doing bobbin-work in the center of flowers, vines, tree trunks and fences adds dimension and texture to any landscape.

TIP: *Do a test sample of the bobbin-work to work out the "kinks" before attempting it on your almost-finished canvas. If your machine is unwilling to do bobbin-work, there are alternatives listed on the next page.*

1. On the Fuse 'n Stitch side of the canvas, use an air soluble marker to draw some undulating lines between the flowers and leaves. You can see the outlines of all of these elements on this side because of the bobbin stitching.

2. Very slowly, by hand, wind one strand of 3-ply, hand-painted cotton floss or pearl cotton around an empty bobbin from left to right until it is 3/4 full. Insert the bobbin into the machine.

3. Select a straight stitch with the stitch length at zero. Thread the top with Sulky 30 wt. Cotton Blendables #4009 Foliage.

TIPS: *Some machines may require the use of an extra bobbin case for the heavy floss. If you have an extra one, loosen the tension screw almost all the way and insert the bobbin; bring the thread through the slit and insert the bobbin case into the machine.*

OR…
You can use your regular bobbin case and by-pass the bobbin tension completely; just bring the floss up through the hole in the bobbin case.

If you need a line to follow for your bobbin work, use a chalk pencil to lightly draw your lines on the black background fabric.

196

4. Place your canvas under the machine needle with the Fuse 'n Stitch side facing up and the embellished side facing down against the machine bed. Hold the top thread while you turn the hand wheel toward you to take one stitch. You will have to pull up hard with the top thread in order to pop the heavier bobbin thread through the fabric. Hold both threads, then run the machine very slowly as you stitch undulating lines. When one section is complete, raise the presser foot, move to the next section, lower the presser foot, and continue. When bobbin work is complete, use a hand sewing needle to pull the threads through to the wrong side, then cut them, leaving about 1-1/2" tails.

Finishing:

1. Using a 1/4" seam allowance, add as many borders as you like to your trimmed piece. Chris chose to add four borders of various widths.

2. The first 2 inner borders were cut 7/8" wide for a finished size of 3/8".

3. The green border was cut 1-1/8" for a finished size of 5/8".

4. The black border was cut 2" for a finished size of 1-1/2".

5. Press the backing fabric. Lay it right side down and spray it with Sulky KK 2000 Temporary Spray Adhesive. Smooth the fleece over it. Spray KK 2000 on the wrong side of the completed Dogwood piece and smooth it over the fleece.

6. Pin the 4 corners with safety pins.

7. Quilt in the ditches using compatible colors of Sulky Blendables®, then stipple stitch as desired.

8. Square up by trimming all sides as needed. Sign your beautiful, completed Dogwood wallhanging.

9. Add the binding. Sulky PolyLite™ 60 wt. Polyester Thread is ideal for hand-sewing the bindings.

5. For the centers of the flowers, stitch in a circular motion very slowly.

NOTE from Editor:

If this technique does not work on your machine, use a couching foot or open-toe appliqué foot to couch the floss down with either the Sulky 30 wt. Cotton #4009 Foliage in the top and bobbin, or Sulky Polyester Clear Invisible in the top and bobbin. Try to achieve the same look as bobbin-work by allowing the floss to be loose and "bunchy" in places. If you need a line to follow, use a chalk pencil to lightly draw your lines on the black background fabric.